SOCIAL
ENTREPRENEURSHIP

KEVIN L. RAWLS, PHD

Kendall Hunt
publishing company

Kendall Hunt
publishing company

www.kendallhunt.com
Send all inquiries to:
4050 Westmark Drive
Dubuque, IA 52004-1840

Published in the United States of America

Dedication

This book is dedicated to the God who has given everyone gifts and talents to serve and love others. I also dedicate this book to my wife and children, who continue to encourage me in my vocation.

Brief Contents

Contents

PART 1: Foundations of Social Entrepreneurship

PART 3: Management of Social Enterprises

PART 4: Financing

Preface

This edition of *Social Entrepreneurship* is meant to be an introductory primer to some of the foundational concepts that surround the practice and study of social entrepreneurship (SE). While there are numerous other publications that offer more in-depth analysis of some of these topics, this book is an attempt to provide a solid basis upon which students of SE can build. Some of the items are ever shifting, such as those related to some of the current legal models, but these should nonetheless serve to provide an awareness of the issues that are impacting the state of SE in the US and globally.

Instructors should find this book to be a good starting point to the study of the topic of SE for their courses. It was written as a footing for an upper-level course in SE, but it would not be out of place in a second-year course for business students, or even non-business majors.

Acknowledgements

I'd like to acknowledge the contribution of my graduate students who helped with the research for this book, William Newlon and Jason Daron. They were invaluable to the completion of this project. I'd also like to thank my writing partner, Dr. Kristen Hark, and the publishing team at Kendall Hunt, Lynne Rogers and Paul Carty. Thank you all for your support.

Introduction

The world around us is changing, and the manner in which we engage in commerce is changing along with it. With the ever increasing amount of information we have access to, and the increasing number of stakeholders in our culture who are impacted by business decisions, our society is looking for ways to bring together conscience and consumption. The rise of social entrepreneurship and social enterprises represents the growth of a business model that leverages market forces for sustained, positive, social impact. This expanded value proposition for products and services recognizes that each business interaction is a part of a larger social fabric, and that can be leveraged to move society forward in a positive and sustainable way.

As you read through this book, keep in mind that social entrepreneurs are not a special group of people with special skills and abilities. They are, however, willing to step forward to engage in business ventures that exist to help others. Social entrepreneurs are those with conviction, who have decided to use their gifts and talents to help make the world around them better. The goal of this book is to help others understand that they can make a change, and that what they start can change the world.

PART 1:

Foundations of Social Entrepreneurship

Chapter 1:

The Search for Definition

Learning Outcomes

- Recognize the primary aspects of social entrepreneurship
- Understand the differences between conventional and social entrepreneurship
- Identify the differences between social entrepreneurship and corporate social responsibility
- Summarize the profit spectrum for social entrepreneurship

Key Terms

Business Model
Conventional Entrepreneurship
Corporate Social Responsibility
For-Profit

Nonprofit
Social Entrepreneurship
Value-Added Transactions

History of Social Entrepreneurship

The term social entrepreneur was first coined by Banks (1972). The early dialogue on social entrepreneurship was focused primarily on understanding how business managers can engage social change by incorporating principles from the business community into social sectors. However, there are hints of social entrepreneurship in literature primarily associated with understanding how business principles can impact social change. The study of social entrepreneurship as an academic discipline really took shape through the work of Gregory Dees (1998). During his time at Stanford and Duke, Dees brought about a greater understanding of the potential for a new way of viewing business, one that focused on value-added interactions for social change, and not just profits.

Social Entrepreneurship

The process of leveraging market demand for goods and services to provide a sustainable, positive change in society.

Gregory Dees Bio

Gregory Dees was one of the leaders in the field of social entrepreneurship and was described by Beth Battle Anderson, one of Dees' closest colleagues, as the "father of social entrepreneurship as an academic field" (Anderson, 2014). Dees received a Bachelor of Arts degree in philosophy from the University of Cincinnati, a master's degree in public and private management from Yale, and a PhD in philosophy from Johns Hopkins University. He was the author of two books titled *Strategic Tools for Social Entrepreneurs: Enhancing the Performance of Your Enterprising Nonprofit* and *Enterprising Nonprofits: A Toolkit for Social Entrepreneurs* as well as numerous journal articles related to this subject. Dees' academic career included positions at the Yale School of Management, Harvard Business School, and the Stanford Graduate School of Business. He finished his career at the Duke University Fuqua School of Business. During his time at Duke University, Dees cofounded the Center for the Advancement of Social Entrepreneurship (CASE), an organization dedicated to providing business leaders and organizations with skills that will help them achieve lasting social impact in their industries. Apart from his academic career, he was also a board member of the Bridgespan Group; an editorial board member of the *Journal of Social Entrepreneurship* and the *Social Enterprise Journal*; and a Chair on the World Economic Forum's Global Agenda Council for Social Innovation. Dees passed away at Duke Hospital at the age of 63.

Anderson, B. B. (n.d.). Remembering Greg Dees (SSIR). (2014, January 9). Retrieved December 04, 2017, from https://ssir.org/articles/entry/remembering_greg_dees

Greg Dees, a Pioneer of Social Entrepreneurship, Dies at Age 63. (2013, December 21). Retrieved December 04, 2017, from https://today.duke.edu/2013/12/gregdees

Another recent example, and a touchpoint event for social entrepreneurship, was Muhammad Yunus winning the Nobel Peace Prize for his work in alleviating poverty through micro loans (Dichter, Katz, Koh, & Karamchandani, 2013). Yunus founded Grameen Bank and developed an innovative way to provide small loans to the poor, many of whom were women. These loans were used to establish small businesses for families, with the goal of lifting individuals up out of poverty. This innovative application of a traditional lending model provides an excellent example of social entrepreneurship in action.

The study of social entrepreneurship is an effort on the part of researchers and scholars to understand the phenomenon of practitioners who engage in innovative and market-oriented solutions to social problems. The literature on social entrepreneurship began to take shape in the late 1990s and early 2000s and has since grown into a robust body of knowledge. Part of the challenge for scholars has been the inability for researchers to settle on a clearly articulated definition of social entrepreneurship. This may seem like a small item, but it is important for those who seek to study a phenomenon to know where the boundaries are in that discipline so that they can clearly isolate and determine the nature of the phenomenon. Even now, twenty years after Gregory Dees seminal work, there are still discussions and disagreements related to the exact definition of social entrepreneurship.

As we begin to study the unique aspects of social entrepreneurship, we focus first on understanding common characteristics of conventional entrepreneurship, in order to better understand the distinctions that might be drawn between conventional and social entrepreneurs. This next section will outline definitions and discussion surrounding the similarities and differences in conventional and social entrepreneurship.

Conventional Entrepreneurship

The efforts of an individual or group to establish a successful business venture from concept to implementation.

Entrepreneurship Overview: Definition and Discussion

Mile High Workshop

©Syda Productions/Shutterstock.com

Mile High WorkShop LLC was formed in 2014 with the mission to "create employment opportunities and provide job training for members of our community seeking to rebuild from addictions, homelessness, and incarceration." They initially attempted to accomplish this by starting several different social enterprises doing various things such as delivering water, making soap, catering events, and making dog beds. They eventually decided to narrow their focus to one section of the supply chain: manufacturing. Instead of focusing on manufacturing one product, they seek out different businesses they can collaborate with. When the company was starting out, most of their customers were production-based small businesses in the Denver area that were in need of increased production. This allowed them to support the local economy as well as provide employment for people with barriers to employment. Although much of their business is still conducted with smaller, local businesses, they have recently been presented opportunities to collaborate with larger companies outside of the local area.

Mile High WorkShop is an example of how mutually beneficial exchanges are successfully achieved in social enterprise. Mile High WorkShop provides support to their small business partners which helps them to grow, and these businesses provide the opportunities and a portion of the funds Mile High WorkShop needs to provide jobs for people with barriers to employment. Although the company is funded partly with donations, it has seen growth toward being completely supported by revenue from its manufacturing services. In a good month they are able to finance 80 percent of their operations using just the revenue from their workshop.

Mile High WorkShop's primary measure of success is whether or not the workers that graduate from their program leave with a job. Someone is considered a graduate if they were with the organization for ninety days or more. The ultimate goal is that these graduates have steady employment and are doing well after they exit the program.

Value-Added Transactions

When we really look at the fundamental basis of business interactions, we tend to think of profits as being the primary motive and driver of business interactions. This is especially true in a free-market system where individuals are free to make decisions related to the use of their income and the mutually beneficial exchange of goods and services (Zupan, 2011). Thus, we are looking at an exchange system where individuals take their money and then spend it in a way best benefiting themselves. However, on an even more fundamental level, businesses exist to create mutually beneficial exchanges. Simply defined, mutual benefit is when an individual exchanges something of value to another individual for the express purpose of determining the relative value of each item (Zupan, 2011). For example, if a person pays $10 for a meal, they are demonstrating that, to them, the meal has a value of at least $10; the restaurant, by pricing the meal at $10, also believes the value of the meal is $10. However, when we look to apply business principles to help solve social problems, we run the risk of possibly little to no exchange value. This is a dynamic typically associated with nonprofits. The Red Cross, for example, is an organization that benefits others, and while the services of the Red Cross are provided to those in need, the people served are not bringing anything of value to the interaction. Conventional entrepreneurship is commonly understood to be the efforts of an individual or group to establish a successful business venture from concept to implementation (Boschee & McClurg, 2003). The conventional entrepreneur measures success by revenue and profits, and seeks to provide a good or service that meets the demand of a particular group or market. The conventional entrepreneur may use an innovative process, technology, or other unique product in such a way as to meet demand in a way that other businesses do not (Bolton & Thompson, 2000).

The discussion of similarities and differences between conventional entrepreneurship and social entrepreneurship activities is pivotal. As we begin to explore some of the unique dimensions and aspects of social entrepreneurship, it is helpful for us to discuss the foundational aspects of entrepreneurship.

Similarities in Structure/Business Model

Business Model

The plan the business has to convert resources to meet market demand for a product or service while taking into account costs and revenue.

Conventional entrepreneurship is focused on finding innovative solutions to meet market demand for goods or services, or to create demand for a new product or service (Sundin, 2011). This type of entrepreneurship is typically associated with a new technology (or new processes) that meets or creates demand in ways previous businesses could not. It is important to note that there are some presuppositions related to economic conditions that must exist prior to entrepreneurial activity; we will discuss these further in future chapters. For the purposes of this particular conventional/social distinction, we assume all of the foundational economic and governmental conditions are met. We will also assume all of the foundational economic and governmental conditions are the same.

Both the conventional and social entrepreneur are interested in new and innovative ways to meet the demand of the end user. Additionally, both the social and the conventional entrepreneur are willing to engage in risk, financial or personal (Nabi & Liñán, 2013). It is also important to note that both models (conventional and social) associate the structure of the organization with the focus of the company. Additionally, both types of entrepreneurial endeavors are focused on long-term viability with an understanding of the relationship between revenue and sustainability.

Distinctions in Structure/Business Model

The conventional entrepreneur and, we will assume by extension, the mission of the company are focused on effectively and efficiently meeting demand and maximizing profits for the company (Ribic, D., 2016; Ribic, I., 2016). When specific business efforts are directly tied to a specific social benefit, we enter the realm of social entrepreneurship.

The conventional entrepreneur measures success and failure by the ability to provide goods or services in such a manner as to create revenue that exceeds business expenses, which are measured in the form of profits. The goal of the company is to maximize the amount of profits for the benefit of the owners. However, the social entrepreneur adds in an additional success measurement: specific social change or a desired social outcome (Boschee & McClurg, 2003). The revenue generated by social enterprise is used to further the goals of the social mission of the company. In other words, profits are not the final measurement of success or failure, there is another aspect that is introduced into the equation—social component or change—which is the ultimate social mission of the company.

The Continuum of Social Entrepreneurship

It is helpful to think about social entrepreneurship and social enterprises as part of a continuum between nonprofit and for-profit institutions. From the chart below, we see space in the middle between purely for-profit companies and those companies relying solely on donations for continued revenue. It is within this mixture of sustainable revenue and social mission that social entrepreneurs operate.

Nonprofit

A tax distinction and governance model that requires an organization to reinvest profits back into the organization.

For-Profit

A tax distinction and governance model that allows an organization to distribute profits to shareholders.

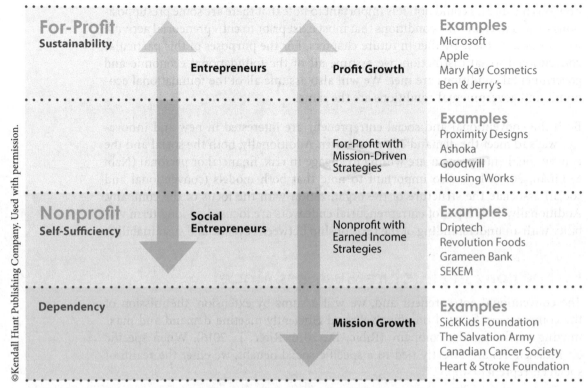

For-Profit
Sustainability

Entrepreneurs

Profit Growth

Examples
Microsoft
Apple
Mary Kay Cosmetics
Ben & Jerry's

For-Profit with
Mission-Driven
Strategies

Examples
Proximity Designs
Ashoka
Goodwill
Housing Works

Nonprofit
Self-Sufficiency

Social
Entrepreneurs

Nonprofit with
Earned Income
Strategies

Examples
Driptech
Revolution Foods
Grameen Bank
SEKEM

Dependency

Mission Growth

Examples
SickKids Foundation
The Salvation Army
Canadian Cancer Society
Heart & Stroke Foundation

Figure 1.1 The entrepreneurship spectrum illustrating the boundaries of social entrepreneurship

Social Entrepreneurship: Overview and Definition

Social entrepreneurship emerged as an effort to bridge the gap between public sector or government-run programs and the social good, combining businesses working to maximize the product efficiency or consumer services (Seelos & Mair, 2005). While there is considerable movement toward a better understanding of the boundaries and scope of social entrepreneurship, it remains a source of debate among academics and practitioners, primarily due to the fact that the methods and language of business do not often fit neatly into the language of social change. Conversely, social change agents do not typically think of their endeavors in terms of ROI, or return on investment, and **value-added transactions**. This difference in definition and language may contribute to the reason social entrepreneurship has appeared to be slow to be adopted into academic institutions. Also, there is little overlap between disciplines focusing on social change, something residing in typically sociologically focused studies, and other disciplines that focus on business and market-oriented programs (Mair & Noboa, 2003). We will see that there are a number of factors affecting increased attention on social entrepreneurship, beginning with the idea of capitalism.

Value-Added Transactions

The measurable benefit to individuals who engage in a market transaction.

Adam Smith is the father of our modern understanding of free market capitalism (Bassiry & Jones, 1993). Smith believed that the ability to freely engage in mutually beneficial transactions allowed space for individuals and businesses to operate efficiently. This model of mutual benefit prevented waste and assured that every business existed to meet the needs of the consumer. Recently, we see Milton Friedman (1970), a modern proponent of free-market capitalism. Friedman asserted that businesses exist as a means of supplying products or services in exchange for some form of currency, allowing people the means and opportunity to be able to purchase those items that they need or want. This particular transaction is focused exclusively on the benefits to the two individuals engaged in the transaction, with little or no focus on the individuals beyond that transaction. This transaction theory offers that the cumulative effect of mutually beneficial transactions has a net benefit on society, as everyone is free to engage in these transactions, allowing everyone to profit as a result of the exchange.

However, there are instances where individuals do not have means or opportunity to obtain items they need, and in a capitalistic system, this has typically been the purview of government (Beed, C., 2015; Beed, C., 2015). Government food programs, for example, provide the needed fundamental supports for citizens who cannot afford basic food items. If an individual finds that they do not have the means to obtain the food they need, the government steps in, offering provision to that individual or family. The government is not bound by the profit maximization and efficiency models constraining typical businesses and can therefore, be prone to inefficient or wasteful practices (Stanbury & Thompson, 1995). What does this look like in the realm of social entrepreneurship? In social entrepreneurship there is a blending of these two goals as social entrepreneurs seek to engage in value-added transactions benefitting the consumer as well as the broader society.

In an effort to consider the impact of transactions on individuals in the larger society, a few theories have emerged. Stakeholder theory and corporate social responsibility emerged to help bring attention to the broader ramifications of individual business transactions to communities, societies, and the world (Baron, 2005; Margolis & Walsh, 2003).

Corporate Social Responsibility

The activities in which an organization shows that they recognize the social impact of their business.

Yellow Tractor

Yellow Tractor LLC partners with businesses and commercial building managers to bring sustainable raised garden beds into their facilities. A purchase from Yellow Tractor includes all materials required to grow the produce, instructions for easy assembly, and access to a wide range of wellness education resources. Wendy Irwin, founder of Yellow Tractor, believes that the best way to impact individuals is to engage them where they spend a large portion of their lives, the workplace. Not only do the employees benefit from the gardens, but they are able to take the fresh fruits and vegetables home and teach their families how to make great tasting, healthy food. The gardens also add value to businesses by encouraging teambuilding and collaboration, and by helping develop a culture of wellness that increases productivity, decreases healthcare costs, and improves employee retention. Yellow Tractor also provides CSR opportunities for businesses by organizing gardening projects that allow employees to engage with their communities.

A portion of the revenue generated by Yellow Tractor goes toward supporting the Yellow Tractor Project, a non-profit branch of the LLC. The Yellow Tractor Project seeks to provide the same products and services as the LLC, but to underserved populations free of charge. A portion of the produce from the gardens in these areas is prepared and served as a snack to children while they are in school. This is very impactful to these students as many of them have never had access to this kind of healthy food. They also organize projects and events in the community including educational series with partner organizations.

Corporate Social Responsibility

The past twenty years have brought about an exponential increase in the amount of information readily accessible to the individual. The Internet and all of its resources not only changed the amount of information available to us, but also changed the way that we access information, and the speed of that access (Dutton & Blank, 2014). And this is true with businesses as well. We have the opportunity, like never before in history, to be made aware of business interactions across the globe in real time. We have the ability to see social impacts along every link in the value chain for a business. For example, we have the ability to know the working conditions of individuals creating and manufacturing electronics goods in Asia. The amount of information is a good thing, as it provides a level of accountability to organizations and businesses that did not previously exist. Organizations also have fewer opportunities to hide, or mask, the impact decisions have on employees and other stakeholders. Additionally, looking at information available to us after the 2008 financial crisis in the United States, we can see how a lack of transparency and a lack of access to information about corporate behavior can have far-reaching, even global, negative ramifications (Mendonca, Galvão & Villela, 2012). Thus, this information can become a burden. What do we as a society do when confronted with information about business activities we believe to be harmful to society? What is the responsibility we bear when given this information?

Access to information not only allows us to know more about corporate activity, but it allows us to be more aware of existing social challenges (Bellow, 2012). We are able to focus on the stories of others, seeing pictures and hearing stories of poverty and need from across the globe; we are forced to resolve the existence of that poverty compared to the concurrent existence of excess and opulence that we observe in others. When confronted with the realities of poverty and need throughout the world, we no longer have the luxury of ignorance, and must resolve the cognitive dissonance arising from the result of our knowledge of suffering. Individuals, and societies, have responded to this previous dissonance by demanding a greater level of awareness about the social impact(s) of business decisions on the part of corporate executives and leaders (Bellow, 2012).

Businesses have responded by placing a greater emphasis on ensuring that the external publics invested in each business are aware of their corporate ethical and socially acceptable practices. The term Corporate Social Responsibility (CSR) is used to describe activities in which an organization shows that they recognize the social impact of their business (Bellow, 2012). We see this acknowledgement of CSR reflected in certain initiatives undertaken by businesses such as donating a certain percentage of proceeds, or profits, to nonprofit or social impact organizations.

It is reasonable to debate the true motives of the corporation or business when they engage in these socially forward activities. Is a business merely trying to put on a facade of social concern in order to give the appearance to the consumer that they are socially conscious, or are they truly trying to use their resources to bring about social change? While it may not be possible to determine the exact motive of these initiatives, the socially driven activities can help provide a social benefit. CSR can be a positive activity and can have a positive impact on the societies in which it is utilized (Eua-anant, Ayuwat & Promphakping, 2011).

CSR, however, is not the same thing as social entrepreneurship, an assumption that many people make. The key difference between the two lies in determining and assessing the true reason a business or organization exists. While there are many successful businesses reaching out to show societal impact—beyond the accumulation of profits—if the social change or societal impact is not part of the core existence and mission of the business, it should not be considered a social enterprise.

A social enterprise or social entrepreneur, places equal or greater value on the social impact rather than profits. In other words, what is the true driver of the business; is it social change at the potential expense of profits, or profits at the expense of social change? The mission of the organization will determine which of these holds more weight in determining the health and goal of the organization. It is important to note that this does not mean that we should not encourage CSR and attempts by conventional businesses and entrepreneurs to encourage social value, but rather, it is an important distinction when we look at the unique qualities of social enterprises and social entrepreneurs.

Additionally, when a corporation, and its shareholders, decide to engage in operations motivated by social change, there is a resulting ethical issue, which Milton Friedman discusses in an article about businesses and social change (1970). The ethical issue arises when an executive of a corporation unilaterally decides to divert revenue or resources to activities that are not directly related to maximizing profits. When an executive does this, he or she is stepping outside the agreed-upon goals of the corporation, which are most often decided upon by the shareholders. The shareholders purchased the shares with the understanding that the motive of the company was to maximize profits. When the executive engages in activities not directly related to that end, they will find themselves in violation of the fiduciary responsibility given to the corporate executive. Again, this can cast doubt on the true motives of executives that engage in CSR, as the fundamental motives of shareholders may not have explicitly changed. It is possible for a corporation motivated exclusively by profit maximization to shift to a social enterprise, but again, this would have to be in coordination with the owners of the business.

References

Abu-Saifan, S. (2012). Social entrepreneurship: definition and boundaries. *Technology Innovation Management Review*, (February), 22–27.

Banks, J.A. (1972). The Sociology of Social Movements. London: MacMillan.

Baron, D. P. (2005). Corporate social responsibility and social entrepreneurship. *Research Paper Series, Research P*, 32.

Bassiry, G. R., & Jones, M. (1993). Adam smith and the ethics of contemporary capitalism. *Journal of Business Ethics, 12*(8), 621. Retrieved from http://ezproxy.liberty.edu/login?url=https://search.proquest.com/docview/198180415?accountid=12085

Beed, C., & Beed, C. (2015). Capitalism, socialism, and biblical ethics. *Journal of Religion and Business Ethics, 3*(1) Retrieved from http://ezproxy.liberty.edu/login?url=https://search.proquest.com/docview/1798316856?accountid=12085

Bellow, E. (2012). Ethical corporate marketing and societal expectations. *Journal of Marketing Development and Competitiveness, 6*(5), 11–26. Retrieved from http://ezproxy.liberty.edu/login?url=https://search.proquest.com/docview/1316073014?accountid=12085

Bolton, B. and Thompson, J. (2000), Entrepreneurs: Talent, Temperament, Technique, Elsevier Butterworth-Heinemann, Oxford.

Bonanno, A., & Goetz, S. J. (2012). Walmart and Local Economic Development. *Economic Development Quarterly*. https://doi.org/10.1177/0891242412456738

Boschee, J., & McClurg, J. (2003). Toward a better understanding of social entrepreneurship: Some important distinctions. *Chief Executive*, 1–5.

Cajaiba-Santana, G. (2014). Social innovation: Moving the field forward. A conceptual framework. *Technological Forecasting and Social Change, 82*(1), 42–51. https://doi.org/10.1016/j.techfore.2013.05.008

Chang, C., & Tuckman, H. (1994). Revenue diversification among non-profits. *Voluntas: International Journal of Voluntary and Nonprofit Organizations, 5*(3), 273–290. Retrieved from http://www.jstor.org/stable/27927443

Clark, G., & Jacks, D. (2007). Coal and the industrial revolution, 1700–1869. *European Review of Economic History, 11*(1), 39–72. Retrieved from http://ezproxy.liberty.edu/login?url=https://search.proquest.com/docview/207331523?accountid=12085

Dees, J. G. (1998). The meaning of social entrepreneurship. *Innovation, 2006*(11-4-06), 1–6. https://doi.org/10.2307/2261721

Dichter, B. S., Katz, R., Koh, H., & Karamchandani, A. (2013). Closing the pioneer gap. Stanford Social Innovation Review, (winter), 36–43.

Dutton, W. H., & Blank, G. (2014). The emergence of next generation internet users. *International Economics and Economic Policy, 11*(1–2), 29–47. http://dx.doi.org/10.1007/s10368-013-0245-8

Eua-anant, P., Ayuwat, D., & Promphakping, B. (2011). Relations between positive impacts of CSR, external support, CSR knowledge and the degree of CSR practices in Thai small and medium enterprises. *The International Business & Economics Research Journal (Online), 10*(11), 17. Retrieved from http://ezproxy.liberty.edu/login?url=https://search.proquest.com/docview/1418717814?accountid=12085

Ferrell, O., Fraedrich, J., & Ferrell, L. (2008). Business Ethics: Ethical Decision-making and Cases. Ohio: South-Western.

Friedman, Milton. 1970. "The Social Responsibility of Business Is to Increase Its Profits." *The New York Times Magazine.* September 13, 1970: pp. 32–33, 122, 126.

Hynes, B. (2009). Growing the social enterprise—issues and challenges. *Social Enterprise Journal, 5*(2), 114–125. http://dx.doi.org/10.1108/17508610910981707

Leadbetter, C. (2014). *The rise of the social entrepreneur. Demos.* Retrieved from www.demos.co.uk

Lehner, O. M., & Nicholls, A. (2014). Social finance and crowdfunding for social enterprises: A public–private case study providing legitimacy and leverage. Venture Capital, *16*(3), 271–286. https://doi.org/10.1080/13691066.2014.925305

Mendonca, H., Galvão, D. J. C., Villela, R.F., (2012). Financial regulation and transparency of information: Evidence from banking industry. *Journal of Economic Studies, 39*(4), 380–397. http://dx.doi.org/10.1108/01443581211255602

Mair, J., & Noboa, E. (2003). Social entrepreneurship: How intentions to create a social enterprise get formed. https://doi.org/10.2139/ssrn.701181

Margolis, J. D., & Walsh, J. P. (2003). Misery loves companies: Rethinking social initiatives by business. *Administrative Science Quarterly, 48*(2), 268–305. https://doi.org/10.1080/10350339209360349

Nabi, G., & Liñán, F. (2013). Considering business start-up in recession time. *International Journal of Entrepreneurial Behaviour & Research, 19*(6), 633–655. Retrieved from http://ezproxy.liberty.edu/login?url=https://search.proquest.com/docview/1445024852?accountid=12085

Nicholls, A. (2009). "We do good things, don't we?": "Blended Value Accounting" in social entrepreneurship. *Accounting, Organizations and Society, 34*(6–7), 755–769. https://doi.org/10.1016/j.aos.2009.04.008

Nicholls, A. (2006). Social Entrepreneurship: New Models for Sustainable Social Change. Oxford

Ribic, D., & Ribic, I. (2016). Social Entrepreneurship. Paper presented at the 18th International Scientific Conference on Economic and Social Development. 287–298. Retrieved from http://ezproxy.liberty.edu/login?url=https://search.proquest.com/docview/1856836894?accountid=12085

Seelos, C., & Mair, J. (2005). Social entrepreneurship: Creating new business models to serve the poor. *Business Horizons, 48*(3), 241–246. https://doi.org/10.1016/j.bushor.2004.11.006

Stanbury, W., & Thompson, F. (1995). Toward a political economy of government waste: First step, definitions. *Public Administration Review, 55*(5), 418. Retrieved from http://ezproxy.liberty.edu/login?url=https://search.proquest.com/docview/197165820?accountid=12085

Sundin, E. (2011). Entrepreneurship and social and community care. *Journal of Enterprising Communities, 5*(3), 212–222. doi: http://dx.doi.org/10.1108/17506201111156689

Wilburn, K., & Wilburn, R. (2014). The double bottom line: Profit and social benefit. *Business Horizons, 57*(1), 11–20. https://doi.org/10.1016/j.bushor.2013.10.001

Zupan, M. A. (2011). The Virtues of Free Markets. *Cato Journal, 31*(2), 171–198. Retrieved from http://ezproxy.liberty.edu/login?url=https://search.proquest.com/docview/875294414?a ccountid=12085

Learning Outcomes

- Identify some of the theories that surround social entrepreneurship research
- Describe the three characteristics of a social enterprise
- Explain the motivation and values of the entrepreneur
- Discuss the profile of the entrepreneur

Key Terms

Agent Theory

Innovation

Market Orientation

Motivation

Social Change Theories

Sociality

Stakeholders

Structuration Theory

Values

Social Impact Theories

Stakeholders

Stakeholder Theory introduces the concept that there are individuals outside of a unique business interaction who have a stake, or are affected in some way, by that interaction. The stakeholder model describes the interactions that exist between a business and those affected by business decisions and opera-

Stakeholders

Those members of a society who are affected by business activity.

tions. Businesses operate within a broader culture, and even individuals who are not directly involved in the exchange have a stake in the company. Those outside of the company can be affected by the activities of the company, whether that affect is a result of the production process, or the implications of the consumption of the goods or services (Ferrell, Fraedrich, & Ferrell, 2008). The stakeholders in a company are considered, among others, customers, employees, suppliers, shareholders, the community, and government regulatory agencies (Ferrell, Fraedrich, & Ferrell, 2008). For example, the employees of the company, while not specifically engaged in the exchange between the goods and services offered by the company and the customer, benefit from that exchange because the money or income produced by that exchange for the company provides the jobs that continue to allow the workers an opportunity for employment.

This broader model of organizational impact has led to a more conscious understanding of how individuals in society are affected by business. When Walmart enters into a town, the price of goods generally drops for everyone, regardless of whether or not they shop at Walmart (Bonanno & Goetz, 2012). Additionally, if a manufacturing company dumps waste into a nearby river and individuals downstream contract different types of diseases—regardless of whether or not they engage in a business transaction with the company—we see stakeholders affected by business activities. In these examples, we see the negative aspects of business activities. When we begin to think about the organization of the greater society, we can begin to develop models for how business interactions can have a positive effect on the stakeholders and the greater society at large, so stakeholder theory contributes to our understanding of social impact. The figure below shows how primary and secondary stakeholders interact with each other and the company.

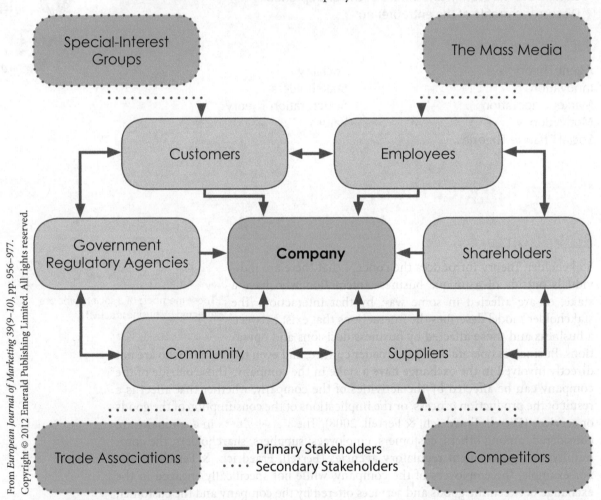

Figure 2.1 Interactions between a company and its primary and secondary stakeholders

Social Change Theory

Social entrepreneurs and enterprises are focused on making fundamental changes to the societies in which they operate. There is a specific need that they believe is not being addressed, and the entrepreneur seeks to impact that need in a unique way. When we look at the interaction between entrepreneurs and the society in which they operate, it is helpful to look at the potential drivers of this type of activity. There are different theories that seek to understand the nature of social movements by trying to explain whether the individual or the social structures are most responsible for change to a society. In other words, who or what is most responsible for social changes.

Social Change Theories

Proposed explanations regarding the forces that precipitate changes in society.

Agent Theory

Agent Theory posits that individuals do break out of socially established structures and seek the change of those structures through creativity and action. Agent Theory provides an explanation for the impact that individuals can have on social change, as they are independent and able to enact change on the social structures in which they operate (Nicholls, 2009).

Agent Theory

A theory that posits that individuals do break out of socially established structures and seek the change of those structures through creativity and action.

Structuration Theory

Structuration Theory places limits on the individual, and confines the activity of the agent to the social forces in which the individual operates (Cajaiba-Santana, 2014). These social structures place boundaries on the impact that an agent can have on the greater social structures around them. A discussion of agents and structuration theory is necessary, as it helps provide an understanding for whether or not the social structure creates the social entrepreneur or whether the social entrepreneur impacts the social structure. This is important as we seek to understand what exactly creates and motivates the social entrepreneur. Is it the idea and the social structures that ultimately prove to be more important to the success of a social entrepreneur, or is it a characteristic or quality that is inherent to the individual? This is vital as we seek to understand whether or not social entrepreneurship be predicted, or developed, in societies or individuals.

Structuration Theory

A belief or policy that places limits on the individual and confines the activity of the agent to the social forces in which the individual operates.

While both of these theories of social change are useful in seeking to point us toward the potential variables that impact social entrepreneurs, it may be helpful to move forward with the assumption that both may be valid, but at varying degrees and varying times. It is true that individuals do exist within certain social structures, and it is challenging to separate the social structures from the individuals who comprise that structure.

Sociality

The aspect of social entrepreneurship that is concerned with the measurable social impact.

Innovation

The dimension of social entrepreneurship concerned with seeking new or more effective ways to solve problems.

Market Orientation

The aspect of social entrepreneurship that seeks to supply goods and services in response to consumer demand.

Theory of Social Entrepreneurship

As we begin to look at defining and setting the parameters of social entrepreneurship, we will focus on three aspects of social entrepreneurship theory as proposed by Nicholls (2009). Social entrepreneurship is focused on the intersection of three dimensions: (1) sociality, (2) innovation, and (3) market orientation. We will begin by looking at each one of these individual areas in more depth.

Sociality

The social component in the term *social entrepreneurship* provides an opportunity to discuss what type of business is considered beneficial to society. Who gets to determine what is beneficial to society? Seeking to identify business outcomes that are exclusively devoted to social change provides challenges. For example, one could make the argument, as Friedman did, that any traditional business exchange is inherently beneficial to society, as you have two individuals who are better off as a result of the exchange. A continuing series of positive exchanges between individuals therefore produces social benefit. What then is unique about the role of the social entrepreneur?

In the social entrepreneurship model, the impact is beneficial to society, both indirectly and directly. In the social enterprise, the impact to the social goals of the company are measured alongside the income goals of the company, both holding weight and value in determining the company's success or failure. So, if a company is meeting their financial goals but not meeting their social goals, adjustments are made to increase the impact or the effectiveness of the social goals. This is considered a double bottom line approach to business success (Wilburn, K., 2014; Wilburn, R., 2014).

Additionally, just because a business has a goal of social change does not mean that change necessarily benefits society. For example, what if an organization existed whose social change goal was to increase the number of individuals addicted to prescription drugs? While not a likely goal of any business, it does emphasize the point that the social goals of an organization might not represent what is in the best interests of society overall. This dynamic can present challenges in determining whether or not a social enterprise or entrepreneurial endeavor is necessarily beneficial to society simply because it has as its main goal, or one of its main goals, social change.

Market Orientation

The second dimension social entrepreneurship is market orientation, described as "the dimension of entrepreneurship that entails rationalizing strategic operations and response to exogenous variables traditionally conceived as competitive market pressures" (Nicholls, 2009, p. 107). When an organization engages in market-oriented activities it means they are looking at demand and exchanges of goods or services, instead of focusing primarily on donations and fundraising activities. By having a market orientation, an organization is forced to focus on efficiency and return on investment with capital and human resources.

However, one of the interesting dynamics of social entrepreneurs and social enterprises is that many of the individuals these organizations are seeking to help may not have the means necessary to afford the products or services offered by the business (Hynes, 2009). Additionally, market-oriented solutions can present ethical challenges as well. For example, an organization may put a product out of reach, through pricing, to those who may most benefit from the product, thereby undermining the very social change the organization is looking to bring about (Hynes, 2009).

Social entrepreneurs should be aware of the potential conflicts that can arise when focusing on goods and services exchanges as a way to create financial sustainability for the organization. This is because there may be cases when the goods or services that are exchanged are incompatible with the desired outcomes of the organization (Lehner & Nicholls, 2014). For example, a social enterprise that sells lottery tickets to help fund the organizational goal of reducing gambling addiction would be engaged in a market orientation that is in conflict with the social goals of the organization. Additionally there can be great temptation for a social enterprise to begin to value the efficient use of resources over the social impact. A social organization that seeks to help low-income individuals obtain meaningful labor might be tempted to reject applicants whose skill set is so low that the resource investment in that individual will likely not produce a return for the organization. It is therefore necessary for a social entrepreneur to take these types of potential conflicts into account as they develop the business model and income-producing strategy for the organization.

REBOOT Recovery

REBOOT was founded with the mission to provide support for combat veterans who are struggling with the effects of PTSD. Many people that return from service continue to face attacks in their mind and spirit, and these struggles can be multiplied if they do not receive the support they need. REBOOT provides a 12-week, faith-based course designed for the veteran's entire family, often provid-ing childcare and a meal. The first stage of the course is designed to provide healing from the trauma that the veterans have received, but it does not end there. REBOOT is dedicated to helping the veterans rebuild strong character, engage in their communities, and reclaim leadership roles. They desire to see veterans move past their program and be equipped to live an abundant life.

REBOOT is focused using philanthropy to subsidize growth not as a source of long term revenue. The consumers of their products are the hosts, and the value they add to the hosts is an opportunity to help change the lives of the veterans around them.

In order for an entrepreneur to develop market-oriented solutions to social problems, it's necessary for them to develop an understanding of value-added transactions and exchanges (Lehner & Nicholls, 2014). What do people need and what are they willing to pay for the product or service? Understanding what people need helps determine demand, and understanding how much they're willing to pay for it helps understand pricing, both of which are necessary characteristics of any sustainable business model. The ability to find new and innovative ways to meet demand is one of the hallmarks of any successful conventional entrepreneur and this is no less the case for the social entrepreneur (Nicholls, 2009). By reducing the need for fundraising and philanthropy, the organization can create a model that is more likely to weather downturns or fluctuations in seasonal giving, as well as be less beholden to the charismatic personality that may be more associated with producing and facilitating charitable giving.

> "Through diversification, nonprofits increase the probability of remaining financially viable by reducing the instability of their funding. Heavy reliance on a single revenue source is seen as imprudent, as in the study of key financial ratios of nonprofit organizations in higher education conducted by Chabotar (1989). (Chang & Tuckman, 1994).

Innovation

What constitutes innovation is a debated topic, and we will review some of the aspects of the debate in this section. It may be natural for us to think of innovation as exclusive to technological advances. For example, the invention of the steam engine was a technological innovation that lead to the industrial revolution (Clark & Jacks, 2007). This type of innovation is an easy-to-point-to example of a technological innovation that made an innovative and substantial contribution to solving problems related to the limits of human and animal labor (Brynjolfsson & McAfee, 2016). Also, we can think of the invention of Facebook as another example of innovation. While the technology may not have been as unique as previous technological innovations, such as the semiconductor, it brought together a number of innovative solutions to social interactions and community engagement. Innovation can be a new model, process, or a technology, but the key is that it is a new way to solve a problem that did not exist previously. The degree of innovation may be subject to debate, but creative problem-solving is a vital component of social entrepreneurship.

Concept-Knowledge Theory

C-K Theory was first introduced by Hatchuel and Weil (2003) who asserted that design could be broken down into two different spaces, concepts and knowledge, and the interaction between the two. Hatchuel and Weil (2009) define the knowledge space (K-space) as an expandable grouping of propositions, either true or false, that describe different objects and the interaction between those objects. In other words, the K-space is the bank of knowledge used by designers in the design process. They define the concept space (C-space) as the compilation of all propositions that have neither a true or false status in the K-space. Therefore, the C-space can be viewed as the collection of all possible solutions to the design problem. C-K Theory seeks to expand on traditional approaches to design by improving the designer's ability to innovate. This innovation happens through the simultaneous expansion of the C-space and K-space. This process is continuous and provides a framework for the design process.

Profile of the Entrepreneur

Behavior

When we look at the social entrepreneur and behavioral profiles of these individuals we take into account both the structure and the agent. Let's move a bit deeper into the profile of the entrepreneur by describing some of their qualities and skills. This combination gives us a richer, more comprehensive view of the person and motivational factors associated with entrepreneurs. Leadbetter (2014) describes some of the qualities of social entrepreneurs, and it is evident that they share these aspects of their skillset and personality with conventional entrepreneurs.

Leadbetter lists social entrepreneurs as being:

- Entrepreneurial: They identify unmet needs or unused resources.
- Innovative: They are creative in problem-solving.
- Transformatory: They move institutions or communities into new dynamics (p. 53).

Additionally, the ability to effectively tell the story of the organization and to lead others toward a common goal are skills that any entrepreneur, social or conventional, would do well to develop in order to move them to success. The storytelling aspect of a social enterprise will be developed in future chapters. Bolton and Thompson (2000) reveal not only do entrepreneurs create products, but they innovate. The process of innovation goes beyond creation in that entrepreneurs will see their ideas come to full fruition, to the end, and overcome barriers that stand in their way.

Many may come to the conclusion that entrepreneurs are more willing to take risks. But this is contrary to what many scholars and research has concluded. It has been shown that entrepreneurs actually view the risk associated with their endeavors at surprisingly lower levels than otherwise thought. Research shows that this is the case because they will focus on the positive potential over the negative potential of their business venture (Nabi & Liñán, 2013).

Motivation and Values

There is a body of research related to the psychological characteristics of the entrepreneur. This is due to the fact that the individual entrepreneur has the potential to move forward an industry or to have broad social impact. Additionally, when we look at the similar manner in which the social (unconventional) entrepreneurs engage in efficiently meeting the needs of the end user, we see similar qualities. The ability to solve problems is a common denominator in both the social and traditional entrepreneur.

Having looked at some key distinctions *between* the conventional and social aspects of entrepreneurship, we now move to an overview of social entrepreneurship. The social entrepreneur is an individual who is driven by a desire to make a change in the world. It is this drive that pushes the individual past obstacles that may have kept others from finding a solution before. This motivation that the social entrepreneur has is built upon a desire to change the world for the better. But why doesn't everyone feel this same desire to make a positive change in the world? What is it about the social entrepreneur that is different? What pushes them to do what they do, and can it be taught or replicated?

Motivation

The driving force behind why an individual engages in certain behavior.

Values

The principles or items that an individual holds as important.

The decisions a person makes are predicated upon a fundamental set of presuppositions that determine how they view the world. These presuppositions on the nature of knowledge, existence, and values, provide the building blocks upon which we all build our worldview. The social entrepreneur possesses a worldview that pushes him or her to value the welfare of others, and to seek out ways to better that welfare, when it is lacking.

Conclusion

When describing the definition and scope of social entrepreneurship, it is important to identify some of the important characteristics of this exciting field. Social entrepreneurship has taken off in the past two decades, thanks to the notoriety of individuals such as Gregory Dees and Mohammed Yunis. By taking the innovative problem-solving of traditional entrepreneurship and devoting it to identified social problems, the social entrepreneur is able to address the needs of others in new and sustainable ways. The theories about social change and the values of the entrepreneur help to provide a foundation upon which we can understand how and why social entrepreneurship is effective. This helps to find ways in which these types of activities can be effectively encouraged and replicated.

References

Abu-Saifan, S. (2012). Social entrepreneurship: definition and boundaries. *Technology Innovation Management Review*, (February), 22–27.

Banks, J.A. (1972). The Sociology of Social Movements. London: MacMillan.

Baron, D. P. (2005). Corporate social responsibility and social entrepreneurship. *Research Paper Series, Research P*, 32.

Bassiry, G. R., & Jones, M. (1993). Adam Smith and the ethics of contemporary capitalism. *Journal of Business Ethics, 12*(8), 621. Retrieved from http://ezproxy.liberty.edu/login?url=https://search.proquest.com/docview/198180415?accountid=12085

Beed, C., & Beed, C. (2015). Capitalism, socialism, and biblical ethics. *Journal of Religion and Business Ethics, 3*(1) Retrieved from http://ezproxy.liberty.edu/login?url=https://search.proquest.com/docview/1798316856?accountid=12085

Bellow, E. (2012). Ethical corporate marketing and societal expectations. *Journal of Marketing Development and Competitiveness, 6*(5), 11–26. Retrieved from http://ezproxy.liberty.edu/login?url=https://search.proquest.com/docview/1316073014?accountid=12085

Bolton, B. and Thompson, J. (2000), Entrepreneurs: Talent, Temperament, Technique. Oxford: Elsevier Butterworth-Heinemann.

Bonanno, A., & Goetz, S. J. (2012). WalMart and Local Economic Development. *Economic Development Quarterly*. https://doi.org/10.1177/0891242412456738

Boschee, J., & McClurg, J. (2003). Toward a better understanding of social entrepreneurship: Some important distinctions. *Chief Executive*, 1–5.

Brynjolfsson, E., & McAfee, A. (2016). The Second Machine Age: Work, Progress, and Prosperity In A Time Of Brilliant Technologies. New York: W. W. Norton.

Cajaiba-Santana, G. (2014). Social innovation: Moving the field forward. A conceptual framework. *Technological Forecasting and Social Change, 82*(1), 42–51. https://doi.org/10.1016/j.techfore.2013.05.008

Chang, C., & Tuckman, H. (1994). Revenue diversification among non-profits. *Voluntas: International Journal of Voluntary and Nonprofit Organizations, 5*(3), 273–290. Retrieved from http://www.jstor.org/stable/27927443

Clark, G., & Jacks, D. (2007). Coal and the industrial revolution, 1700–1869. *European Review of Economic History, 11*(1), 39–72. Retrieved from http://ezproxy.liberty.edu/login?url=https://search.proquest.com/docview/207331523?accountid=12085

Dees, J. G. (1998). The meaning of social entrepreneurship. *Innovation, 2006*(11-4-06), 1–6. https://doi.org/10.2307/2261721

Dichter, B. S., Katz, R., Koh, H., & Karamchandani, A. (2013). Closing the pioneer gap. Stanford Social Innovation Review, (winter), 36–43.

Dutton, W. H., & Blank, G. (2014). The emergence of next generation internet users. *International Economics and Economic Policy, 11*(1–2), 29–47. http://dx.doi.org/10.1007/s10368-013-0245-8

Eua-anant, P., Ayuwat, D., & Promphakping, B. (2011). Relations between positive impacts of CSR, external support, CSR knowledge and the degree of CSR practices in thai small and medium enterprises. *The International Business & Economics Research Journal (Online), 10*(11), 17–n/a. Retrieved from http://ezproxy.liberty.edu/login?url=https://search.proquest.com/docview/1418717814?accountid=12085

Ferrell, O., Fraedrich, J., & Ferrell, L. (2008). Business Ethics: Ethical Decision making and Cases. Ohio: South-Western.

Friedman, Milton. 1970. "The Social Responsibility of Business Is to Increase Its Profits." The New York Times Magazine. September 13, 1970: pp. 32–33, 122, 126.

Hatchuel, A., & Weil, B. (2003). A New Approach of Innovative Design: an Introduction To C-K Theory. *DS 31: Proceedings of ICED 03, the 14th International Conference on Engineering Design*, (June), 1–15. https://doi.org/citeulike-article-id:4891368

Hatchuel, A., & Weil, B. (2009). C-K design theory: An advanced formulation. *Research in Engineering Design, 19*(4), 181–192. https://doi.org/10.1007/s00163-008-0043-4

Hynes, B. (2009). Growing the social enterprise - issues and challenges. *Social Enterprise Journal, 5*(2), 114–125. http://dx.doi.org/10.1108/17508610910981707

Leadbetter, C. (2014). *The rise of the social entrepreneur. Demos.* Retrieved from www.demos.co.uk

Lehner, O. M., & Nicholls, A. (2014). Social finance and crowdfunding for social enterprises: A public–private case study providing legitimacy and leverage. Venture Capital, *16*(3), 271–286. https://doi.org/10.1080/13691066.2014.925305

Mendonca, H., Galvão, D. J. C., Villela, R.F., (2012). Financial regulation and transparency of information: Evidence from banking industry. *Journal of Economic Studies, 39*(4), 380–397. http://dx.doi.org/10.1108/01443581211255602

Mair, J., & Noboa, E. (2003). Social entrepreneurship: How intentions to create a social enterprise get formed. https://doi.org/10.2139/ssrn.701181

Margolis, J. D., & Walsh, J. P. (2003). Misery loves companies : Rethinking social initiatives by Business. *Administrative Science Quarterly, 48*(2), 268–305. https://doi.org/10.1080/10350339209360349

Nabi, G., & Liñán, F. (2013). Considering business start-up in recession time. *International Journal of Entrepreneurial Behaviour & Research, 19*(6), 633–655. Retrieved from http://ezproxy.liberty.edu/login?url=https://search.proquest.com/docview/1445024852?accountid=12085

Nicholls, A. (2009). "We do good things, don't we?': "Blended Value Accounting" in social entrepreneurship. *Accounting, Organizations and Society, 34*(6–7), 755–769. https://doi.org/10.1016/j.aos.2009.04.008

Nicholls, A. (2006). Social Entrepreneurship: New Models for Sustainable Social Change. Oxford.

Ribic, D., & Ribic, I. (2016). Social Entrepreneurship. Paper presented at the 287–298. Retrieved from http://ezproxy.liberty.edu/login?url=https://search.proquest.com/docview/1856836894?accountid=12085

Seelos, C., & Mair, J. (2005). Social entrepreneurship: Creating new business models to serve the poor. *Business Horizons, 48*(3), 241–246. https://doi.org/10.1016/j.bushor.2004.11.006

Stanbury, W., & Thompson, F. (1995). Toward a political economy of government waste: First step, definitions. *Public Administration Review, 55*(5), 418. Retrieved from http://ezproxy.liberty.edu/login?url=https://search.proquest.com/docview/197165820?a ccountid=12085

Sundin, E. (2011). Entrepreneurship and social and community care. *Journal of Enterprising Communities, 5*(3), 212–222. http://dx.doi.org/10.1108/17506201111156689

Wilburn, K., & Wilburn, R. (2014). The double bottom line: Profit and social benefit. *Business Horizons, 57*(1), 11–20. https://doi.org/10.1016/j.bushor.2013.10.001

Zupan, M. A. (2011). The Virtues of Free Markets. Cato Journal, *31*(2), 171–198. Retrieved from http://ezproxy.liberty.edu/login?url=https://search.proquest.com/docview/875294414?a ccountid=12085

Chapter 3

The Environment of Social Entrepreneurship

Learning Outcomes

- Become familiar with the cultural drivers of social entrepreneurship
- Understand the political systems that seem to foster social entrepreneurship
- Explain how consumer behavior affects the increase or the success of social enterprises
- Use these drivers to begin to understand and identify opportunity recognition

Key Terms

Consumer Values
Credit
Culture
Economic Conditions
Inverse Demand

Markets
Political System
Social Values
Voluntary Exchange

Cultural Context for Social Entrepreneurship

Three Sisters

Three Sisters is an L3C organization founded with the purpose of producing fashion items in Benin, a small country in western Africa, and using the revenue generated by the sale of those products to support the communities where they were produced. One of the main ways they administer this support is through the TS Education Fund, which provides tutoring services in French, chemistry, mathematics, and English to children ages four to nineteen. These

©Anton_Ivanov/Shutterstock.com

tutoring sessions are conducted in the homes of the students so that not only the students receive the benefits, but parents, who may have never received the education, can also benefit from them. One of the major issues they ran into was that children in the lowest economic conditions were the ones that would miss tutoring sessions most often. They found that this was happening due to the need for these children to spend the time they could be in tutoring out trying to make money for their family to survive. This has caused Three Sisters to continually look for new ways to provide these children with financial resources so they can attend their tutoring sessions.

Approximately 20% of the funding Three Sisters receives comes from the sale of earrings, headbands, and other forms of jewelry that are produced by artisans in Benin. However, conducting this business in Benin brings up a few issues. One of these issues is supply-chain management. Since Benin is located so far from the United States, it can be hard to monitor the suppliers of their products to ensure that the goods are being produced in the way Three Sisters wants them to be produced. One example of this is the use of child labor, which goes against Three Sisters' mission to educate children and give them an opportunity for a better future. Supply-chain issues are not only geographic, but also political and cultural. For example, another issue that has recently surfaced is the possibility for trade agreements to shift. Currently, Three Sisters is not required to pay import taxes on items produced in Benin. However, if this were to change they would be required to reevaluate their pricing strategy. Also, communication can be an issue since the people they connect with speak French, English, and multiple local languages. This can make doing business difficult because business terms and concepts can often be difficult to translate.

Another 15 percent of Three Sisters' funding comes from Books that Bind. Books that Bind started as a class project at Michigan State University, where cofounder Dr. Marcy O'Neil is an assistant professor and advisor. In this project, folktales told in Benin were recorded and translated, giving the children in the Three Sisters Education Fund Program the opportunity to create books that reflect their culture. These books can be purchased on the Three Sisters website and come with resources that explain what the stories mean and why they were written. They have also adopted a buy-one, give-one model where for each book purchased, one book is donated to a school library in Benin.

Political System

The method of governance in place in a particular population that enacts and enforces laws.

Culture

The collective social values and systems in which a market operates.

As with any business activity, the exchanges do not take place in a vacuum, but in the larger context of a social, economic, and political system. This chapter will look at some of the broader systems that can have an impact on the social entrepreneur. The manner in which social change occurs and the nature of the models that exist in that culture both play a part in how a social entrepreneur operates and succeeds. For this chapter, we will take a cross-cultural approach to this assessment, meaning that each one of these is a variable that may differ from one culture or one country to the next. This represents a framework through which we can assess the environment in which entrepreneurial activity, specifically social entrepreneurship, can function and thrive the best (Morris, 1995).

While these components may be fairly well understood by an entrepreneur in the context of the United States, it is important to realize the underlying factors and how they can change in a variety of different contexts. Each of these components represents an opportunity for a globally minded social entrepreneur to impact a society, but in a more fundamental and paradigm-shifting way.

Economic

When we discuss the macroeconomic factors of a culture we are looking at the broader systems of exchange that operate in a given society. For example, a free-market system places a greater emphasis on the individual decisions of consumers and producers, and a more socialist system tends to centralize these decisions in the role of a government or civic structure. The means of consumption and production, and the freedom that an individual has to choose these means, is a fundamental component of macroeconomic systems.

While there is no economic system that is perfect and able to fully account for every possible human need and suffering in an effective and efficient way, it is typically the more free-market and capitalist systems that allow for the rise of entrepreneurs able to combat these gaps in meeting the needs of the populace (Morris & Lewis, 1995). It is due to the fact that individuals have the chance and the opportunity to engage in new and innovative ways to solve problems. This allows for these those individuals who slip through the cracks in the system to be effectively, efficiently, and immediately tended to. It is even argued that free markets promote ethics and values that other markets do not. The reason for this is because, in a free market, how one behaves and deals with others in the present will result in how well off they are in the future. Free markets encourage mutually beneficial exchanges which benefit society as a whole. Rather than corrupt economies, which focus on individuals trying to work their way up the economic ladder while sometimes taking very unethical actions, free-market economies promote mutually beneficial exchanges (Zupan, 2011). But this is not to suggest that everyone in the capitalist, free-market society is looking to better society as a whole; there is still room for dysfunction to occur with unethical people. It is important to have both ethical consumers and producers for a free market to fully flourish (Bassiry & Jones, 1993).

We also have to keep in mind that it is ultimately on the value system of the entrepreneur whether or not these individuals on the margins of society are effectively taken care of and addressed, even in a more closed governmental and economic system. These individuals may exist, but the population might not have the freedom, the opportunity, and the chance to be able to address those needs appropriately.

It is also helpful to begin to look at some of the primary drivers of economic development, as these represent opportunities for social entrepreneurs to seek out ways in which they can use disruptive activities to advance social missions. Schumpter (2012) lists a number of activities that propel forward economic development:

- The introduction of a new good, or a new quality of a good
- The introduction of a new method of production
- The opening of a new market
- The conquest of a new source of supply of raw materials or half-manufactured goods
- The carrying of the new organization of any industry, such as breaking up or establishing a monopoly (p. 66)

These activities are tied to economic development and are opportunities for entrepreneurial activity on the part of a socially conscious producer. It is also worth noting that the movement forward is driven primarily by the producers, rather than the consumers, as the force of change in the economic movement of a society. As the means of production are able to be employed by a greater number of those in society, there exists more opportunity for innovative activities to take place (Schumpeter, 2012).

Political

The system of government that is in place in a state or country has an impact on the ways in which social entrepreneurship operates and why it exists at all. One of the pillars of successful social entrepreneurship is the ability of an individual to begin a business and to own private property. This dynamic is taken for granted in many parts of the western world, but it is not a condition that is shared by all those around the globe. There are other systems of government where only a certain part of the populace is allowed to own property, and these systems may exclude women or minorities by preventing them from engaging in business ownership (Morris & Lewis, 1995).

Economic Conditions

The financial state of a country or region.

When assessing the political climate in which social entrepreneurship operates, it is important to take into account not just the political system, but also the impact that the political system has on the economics of a country. This is due to the fact that the political system is primarily devoted to the enforcement of laws, but also a certain amount of wealth redistribution. Many of the most socially challenging areas are those that are a result of unequal or disproportional economic conditions between various strata of citizens.

If these conditions are the result of political and economic systems, then the society will impact the manner in which a social entrepreneur addresses change. If individuals are not allowed to have the freedom to make individual choices as to where they purchase goods, it will affect the type of product or service that the social entrepreneur offers. Additionally, the ability for a system to have a stable and predictable currency policy will have an effect on exchanges that take place within a country or state.

The ability for an individual or an organization to keep the profits from an entrepreneurial activity is also a key component of the environment. This is due to the fact that, if individuals are not allowed to benefit from the profits of an organization, then there is less motive to engage in the risk that naturally comes with entrepreneurial activity.

Additionally, the legislative system of the country can impact the social enterprise when it comes to the ability to predict the stability of laws or policies related to business or organizational ownership. If a legislative system is highly centralized and subject to the changes of a small group of people, those individuals may choose to make swift changes to the laws that affect social enterprises. This makes having a long-term sustainable business model a challenge (Morris & Lewis, 1995).

DoorDash and Feeding America

There is a difference between the amount of food that is produced each year and the amount of food that is consumed. In the ideal world, the amount of food consumed would equal the amount produced, but this ultimately is an impossible task to accomplish. One new partnership between DoorDash and Feeding America, known as ReFED, and legislation in New York are attempting to reduce the nearly 58 million tons of food wasted each year and the one in seven US citizens lacking nutritious food. ReFED has hopes to reduce the amount of food wasted in half by the year 2030. ReFED has released a Retail Food Waste Action Guide to instruct grocery retailers in coming up with and implementing new strategies for reducing food waste (Sustainable Brands, 2018).

DoorDash, a restaurant delivery service, has partnered with Feeding America. DoorDash is undergoing a pilot program to help deliver excess food from restaurants to food banks. Additionally, there is legislation in the works to help bridge the excess food and poverty gap in New York. Governor Andrew Cuomo is working to on a recycling law that would require organizations to arrange for the recovery and recycling of excess food and scraps if they produce more than two tons of it a week (Sustainable Brands, 2018).

Sustainable Brands. (2018, January 26). Trending: New Tools, Rules, Partnerships Take Food Waste, Hunger Head On. Retrieved February 02, 2018, from http://www.sustainablebrands.com/news_and_views/waste_not/sustainable_brands/trending_new_tools_rules_partnerships_take_food_waste_hu

Legal

The judicial system also impacts the way in which social entrepreneurs and enterprises operate, as the ability to protect intellectual property might be a core component of the business model. If intellectual property rights are not protected by a legislative and judicial system, then the opportunity to have that property as an asset or competitive advantage may not be an option for that organization, which may in turn affect sustainability. Also, the ability to enforce and create mutually beneficial contracts is a component of a supply chain for many enterprises. If that process is subject to impact by bribes or the shifting loyalties of the legal authorities, it can affect the model and sustainability of the organization.

The concept of voluntary exchange is a way that describes the freedom that individuals have to exchange goods or services in a way. Voluntary exchange means that each individual in an economic system is allowed to decide whether or not to purchase one good or service over another. This brings in a couple of concepts that are worth exploring. One is the idea of competition, and the other is the idea of individual freedom of choice. Competition is a concept that is a part of a free-market system of exchanges.

> **Voluntary Exchange**
>
> An event in which an individual or group has the freedom to make exchanges of goods or services in accordance with their wants or needs.

Peaceful Fruits

Peaceful Fruits LLC produces fruit snacks that use ingredients that are hand-harvested by local farmers in the Amazon Rainforest. Founder Evan Delahanty developed the idea for peaceful fruits while volunteering in the United States Peace Corps in Suriname, a country in northeastern South

©Ricardo D'Almeida/Shutterstock.com

America. Evan observed that life can be very hard for the people living in the remote areas of this country, and they often have to make tough decisions about how to provide for themselves and their family. Since acai is already a commodity that is traded all over the world, they did not have to create the market from scratch. However, creating a system that enables the locals to harvest fresh fruits from the forest for a fair wage supports sustainable economic development, which helps improve the lives of the people in these areas.

Evan has also found that the scale of Peaceful Fruits has presented a few issues. Developing a supply system with the limited financial resources available would have been incredibly difficult, if not impossible. Therefore, to obtain the materials they need to produce their product, they partner with businesses that already have the supply systems in place. Peaceful Fruits then focuses on developing their brand and getting their product to customers. However, finding partners can be difficult because larger corporations that supply these materials often don't want to distribute the smaller quantities that Peaceful Fruits' capacity requires. Their long-term goal is to set up their own production facility in Suriname.

Financial

Markets

Areas that facilitates the exchange of goods or services between individuals or groups.

Access to **markets** is an important part of any entrepreneurial endeavor and social enterprises are no different. The ability to be able to find the markets that have the most demand for a product is key, for if there is no market then there is no way for the goods or services to be sold. This is true of national and international businesses. One of the most important contributions of the ever-increasing globalized society is the ability for a small company to have access to markets on the other side of the world. This increase in market availability allows an organization to meet demand for a product, regardless of geographic location (Stela, 2013). Additionally, e-commerce puts the information about these organizations at the fingertips of anyone in the world, and allows them to operate in the same way as a much larger firm, as they are both accessed through the same medium. This dynamic diminishes some of the advantage that is typically associated with large stores that own prime real estate in high-traffic areas, which are a traditional advantage to a brick-and-mortar store.

Availability of Credit

Credit

The ability to have access to goods or services on the condition of future payment.

Additionally, the availability of **credit** is a vital component of entrepreneurial activity (Schumpeter, 2012). The opportunity to access financing for new ventures is a key component, as it expands the innovative capacity beyond those who are already established as owners of wealth, and makes innovation available to a greater number of people, thereby releasing the entrepreneurial activities to a greater percentage of the population (Schumpeter, 2012).

This is an important concept to understand, and it is not one that we typically associate with entrepreneurial activity, social or conventional. However, we can see in the successors of Muhammed Yunis (Grameen-info.org), and the micro-lending initiatives that he established in Bangladesh, that the availability of credit, even in a small amount, can allow innovation to occur in every aspect of the socioeconomic conditions of a country.

Grameen Bank was founded in 1983 by Muhammed Yunis as a way to begin to provide credit to some of the poorest citizens of Bangladesh without the lenders having to provide collateral. The result was that lower-income citizens had access to the kind of capital that allowed them to start their own businesses and to pay back the loans from the success of those businesses. The primary beneficiaries were women, as they accounted for 97% of the loan recipients. These "micro-loans" were paid back as lower interest rates, so the repayments were not so burdensome as to inhibit the growth of the small businesses.

http://www.grameen-info.org/

Entrepreneurial activity needs investment capital, and it is access to this capital that is necessary for social entrepreneurs to thrive. As was the case with Grameen Bank, the absence of the availability of credit in a society can present an opportunity for a social entrepreneur to not only engage in an activity that positively affects the recipient of the funds, but can also have a broader outcome for an entire society.

Social Structures

Social structures represent the various aspects of culture in which businesses and other organizations operate. The various social structures in a culture can be assessed in a number of ways; however, we will select a few of most relevant to the topic of social entrepreneurship. In the following sections we will look at each one of these in turn.

Education

The status of a culture's educational system can tell us much about the way in which information and cultural values are disseminated in a society (Satterlee, 2018). Formalized educational systems allow for unified and consistent communication across cultures. It is also relevant to understand if there are any unique conditions in order to be educated in a particular culture. For example, in many cultures women are not allowed to formally enter school. Understanding this dynamic and how it impacts opportunities for social entrepreneurs, as well as limitations for cultural social entrepreneurship, is vital to understanding how social entrepreneurship can be successful in a culture. Additionally entrepreneurial principles can be most effectively communicated to the population of a country through a formalized educational system, as it helps provide a consistent and regulated method of education and information dissemination. Also, the existence of a formalized education system is the outcome of a number of other important considerations such as a well-funded civic oversight system or government, and the existence of a communication system that is both written and communicable. We will look at this communication aspect of culture in the next section.

Communication: Language

As with the other items addressed in this section of the chapter, we cannot assume that a common language exists in every economic system. To show this point, there are over forty different languages in Kenya (Thomley, Wood, Grace, & Sullivant, 2011).

We have the luxury here in the United States of a relatively homogeneous communication and language structure. And this common language allows for business transactions to move with relative ease. However, that is not the case in all areas of the world. Language acts as a stabilizer to a country, and different languages can represent an inhibiting factor to business transactions and decisions. This is especially true of the impact that values systems and culture have on a country, or an economic system. The common language allows culture to distribute and spread consistently across a region.

This is because, in a practical sense, the impact of translation can be a burden on business interactions, even impacting units of measurement, monetary systems, and consumer behavior. If the language is common in a culture, it makes entrepreneurial activity more effective, and more likely to occur. This may be especially true for social entrepreneurs, as one of the key components of addressing social change is the ability to obtain buy in from the consumers. The ability to communicate and tell the story and express the issues associated with particular social problem can be spread much more easily in a culture that shares a common language.

Religion and Worldview

Social Values

Those principles that a society deems as important and worthy of high regard.

The impact of religion and worldview plays a role in the environment of social entrepreneurship as it can impact the way in which individuals assess needs and the perceived moral obligation to act in a certain way toward those needs. For example, in a culture that views the suffering of another person as a spiritual punishment for past lives, that person is likely to be seen as reaping what they have sown and others may be less inclined to perceive their situation as a need that must be addressed. However, if a cultural religious tradition sees those who suffer as individuals in need of assistance and who came about their situation through no fault of their own, then others may feel compelled to take steps to alleviate the suffering. The social value of each individual, as well as the society as a whole, is a necessary component for effective social entrepreneurship activities (Albert, Dean & Baron 2016). Religion is one of the primary drivers of cultural values as it provides a rationale and a justification for why certain values are to be upheld as desirable, and certain behaviors are to be avoided. This is the foundation for a country's legal system as well as the behavior of consumers and producers in a region. Cultural values are handed down from generation to generation in family structures, as well as formal educational institutions. and these values are primarily derived from the religious system that is in place in a culture.

This aspect also has a practical component as it is important for a social structure and the social stratification of a society to value to the individual, as social "walls" that separate one class from another lose the benefit of networking and of the innovation that can come from the mixing of skills and talents that are available from a more diverse social group. The greater freedom that individuals have to engage in productive dialogue and activity with others is a vital component for the advancement of common social entrepreneurial activity (Morris & Lewis, 1995). Social stratification can express itself in a variety of ways. Societies can be stratified along gender lines, with certain cultures valuing the contributions of men more than women, and the resulting laws or systems that reflect those values drive the economic realities of each group. A country can also develop along economic lines, with higher income being of more value than lower incomes.

It is also impactful on a society whether or not certain social placement is arranged through birthright, or whether different social roles can be obtained through effort and achievement. It is not a stretch to see the impact that this can have on entrepreneurial activity because the ability of an individual to create change is a key component for the entrepreneur in motivating them to action. If a social system is preventative of individual achievement or movement from one level to another, it might prove an inhibitor to entrepreneurial activity.

Additionally, when we look at how cultural values impact entrepreneurship, and specifically social entrepreneurship, we can see how gender differences are affected by who is able to engage in the workforce and who is able to engage in entrepreneurial activity. The ability of half of the population, or up to half the population, to be excluded from entrepreneurial activity prevents a substantial amount of gifts, talents, and skills from being engaged in the pursuit of social entrepreneurship and social outcomes. However, this in itself presents an opportunity for social enterprises to exist as a mechanism for moving culture from one that does not empower and enable women to be entrepreneurs to one that does value them. Nevertheless, the underlying cultural values that prevented it to begin with must be addressed, and must be substantially changed, in order for progress to be made in this.

It is the producers that fundamentally drive economic development and innovation. It is in the meeting of consumer demand that forces the producers to engage in activities that move forward new and innovative ways to produce goods that are different or provide higher consumer value that creates the change that moves for development. The demand from the consumer might prompt the innovation, but it is the production of the materials that really creates the change in the product or service, which provides the economic impact to the value chain.

Parker Clay LLC

Parker Clay founders Ian and Brittney Bentley developed a passion for helping the millions of orphans worldwide. This led them to Ethiopia where they witnessed many young women and children with no opportunity or education be forced into prostitution or slavery. It was through these experiences, and their interactions with organizations seeking to empower these women, that they developed the idea for Parker Clay. Parker Clay LLC produces luxury lifestyle goods from leather and hand-woven textiles, as well as jewelry products, by hiring vulnerable women crafters in Ethiopia. These jobs provide women with the means to support their families and further their mission to transform communities through economic and social empowerment. Parker Clay also partners with an Ethiopian nonprofit named Ellilta—Women at Risk, which supports these women through relationship-based recovery methods.

Ian and Brittney observed that some customers are compelled by their story to purchase their products. However, they found that many people only hear about their story after they have purchased their products. They attribute this to their dedication to provide high quality products rather than solely relying on their story to sell their products.

Consumer Behavior

The priorities of the consumer are a necessary consideration when assessing the broader cultural impacts on social entrepreneurship. If a culture has a strong desire to receive the maximum amount of financial return on an investment, then they may be less likely to value the social impact of a specific purchasing decision or investment.

Conversely, if a consumer culture values the social impact of a decision, then that will affect the business model that a social entrepreneur chooses to pursue. In societies that place great emphasis on social impact, it is important that the entrepreneur is aware of the expectations that are upon them from society. It is vital to the success of the organization that they are conscious of the social impact that their company is expected to have. For example, if the society places a lot of emphasis on green initiatives, it is crucial for the entrepreneur to understand and adapt their business plan to that expectation (Bellow, 2012).

As with any business exchange, the goal is to maximize the value for the consumer as well as the producer. The social entrepreneur begins to see value beyond financial return and looks to add value in ways that may not be as tangible but are no less real. We see this dynamic already when we look at the value that a consumer places on a specific brand. The brand that is being purchased is as important, if not more, than the functional value of the item itself. While one watch may function the same way as another, the brand name on one will increase the value, and the price of that item reflects that value. In an environment where a social enterprise succeeds it is important to understand how the consumers value social contribution and consumerism. A customer base that values personal consumption at the expense of social good may be less likely to consume products that are tied to a specific social value. However, the opposite is also true. A customer base that places a high value on social or environmental responsibility will value exclusively personal consumption less.

We can see in the United States that the values of the consumer have had an impact on the producers in our country, as there is a rise in products that incorporate into their marketing a socially-conscious component (Kerlin, 2006). This consumer behavior has driven producers to look for innovative ways to shift resources and strategies to meet the expectations of consumers to engage in consumption that is consistent with their values (Abert, Dean & Barron, 2016). This dynamic has always been the case, as consumption always reflects consumer values, but it is a shift toward a consumer value system that wants to make a social difference. That has led to the new paradigm.

Consumer Values

The principles or items that consumers regard as important.

A number of different psychological and social factors have led to this shift, but it is necessary for a social entrepreneur to be aware that if they are to create a new process or product that seeks to meet market demand, they must understand what the consumers value in a given society.

Infrastructure

The existence of a well-established infrastructure system is something that we might take for granted in the west. The ability to move goods to other geographic areas, as well as the ability for individuals to establish careers or personal goals in areas outside of where they grew up, is not present in every other area of the world. The impact that the interstate and highway system has had on the economic development in the United States is difficult to understand it.

Additionally, a system of providing electricity to citizens that are spread out over geographic area allows for productivity to increase among the population. Again, as with other aspects of the social entrepreneurship environment, infrastructure provides the foundation as well as an opportunity for social entrepreneurs. In areas of the world where these types of infrastructure components are not in place, it provides an opportunity for the social entrepreneur to move in and creatively develop ways in which this infrastructure can be established. For example, a team of social entrepreneurs in India sought to use discarded rice husks as a source for powering generators that could produce electricity for areas of India that did not have the service (Dichter, Katz, Koh, & Ashish, 2013). Again, this group of social workers sought to establish the infrastructure necessary for continued economic development and entrepreneurship in a creative and socially beneficial way. Once infrastructure is in place it allows for other social entrepreneurs to come in and "move the ball forward" through innovation that maximizes this infrastructure for social benefit.

Market Demand

An interesting aspect of social entrepreneurship and enterprise is the unique way in which demand is assessed. This is due to the dynamic that exists in a conventional enterprise versus a social enterprise. When a conventional entrepreneur looks at a market opportunity, they are looking at either meeting an existing demand, or they are looking to create a demand through the introduction of a new product or service.

However, the social entrepreneur views market demand in a unique way. Not only do they have to view demand from the traditional sense, as they are looking at engaging the market in an effort to create a sustainable model of revenue, but they can also view the social impact they are seeking to make as a type of demand. For example, if there is a social entrepreneur who is seeking to alleviate hunger in a particular region, he or she can see the existence of hunger as a type of "demand" that should be addressed. However, unlike the conventional entrepreneur, the social entrepreneur does not look to increase or create demand, but instead they are seeking to decrease the demand of hunger. This could be considered an "inverse demand" model for the social enterprise. This demand model is unique to the social entrepreneur.

Opportunity Recognition

We will discuss this further in future chapters, but understanding some of the primary drivers and the environment in which entrepreneurial activity thrives is a necessary component to understanding what allows this type of activity to succeed. It also assists with opportunity recognition, in that the absence of these drivers can provide a social entrepreneur with a place to start when looking at impacting a society in a positive way. For example, if a country does not have a strong infrastructure, than the absence of that aspect of economic activity can provide the social entrepreneur with a place in which they can make a difference in the entire society.

Additionally as an individual entrepreneur seeks to impact a particular culture or social structure, it is important that they take into account all of the environmental factors that may be truly responsible for the problem, as this will determine what the social entrepreneur may need to address to solve it. For example, if there is a particular community that is dealing with a low level of employment, it may be that they are unable to obtain jobs due to being a member of a lower social class. If that is the case, then the social entrepreneur will address that problem differently than if the issue is a lack of transportation to the areas where jobs are located.

Conclusion

Any business interaction takes place within the context of a broader social and cultural reality. It is necessary for any social entrepreneur to understand the fundamental cultural identity of the society in which they are seeking to change and do business. Additionally, understanding the social structures can help a social entrepreneur to understand some of the issues that may be driving the social need, such as disproportionate educational opportunities, and inherent bias against specific members of the society. These types of fundamental issues go to the broader understanding of not only the outcomes of social Enterprise but also the larger impact that they should seek in the society, which will result in the long-term fundamental change of the culture.

References

Albert, L. S., Dean, T. J., & Baron, R. A. (2016). From social value to social cognition: How social ventures obtain the resources they need for social transformation. *Journal of Social Entrepreneurship, 676*(June), 1–23. https://doi.org/10.1080/19420676.2016.1188323

Bassiry, G. R., & Jones, M. (1993). Adam Smith and the ethics of contemporary capitalism. *Journal of Business Ethics, 12*(8), 621. Retrieved from http://ezproxy.liberty.edu/login?url=https://search.proquest.com/docview/198180415?accountid=12085

Bellow, E. (2012). Ethical corporate marketing and societal expectations. *Journal of Marketing Development and Competitiveness, 6*(5), 11–26. Retrieved from http://ezproxy.liberty.edu/login?url=https://search.proquest.com/docview/1316073014?accountid=12085

Dichter, B. S., Katz, R., Koh, H., & Karamchandani, A. (2013). Closing the pioneer gap. *Stanford Social Innovation Review,* (winter), 36–43.

Grameen Bank. Retrieved from http://www.grameen-info.org/

Kerlin, J. A. (2006). Social enterprise in the United States and Europe: Understanding and learning from the differences. *Voluntas: International Journal of Voluntary and Nonprofit Organizations, 17*(3), 247–263. https://doi.org/10.1007/s11266-006-9016-2

Morris, M. H., & Lewis, P. S. (1995). The determinants of entrepreneurial activity Implications for marketing, *29*(7), 31–48.

Satterlee, B. (2018). Cross Border Commerce. Richland, WA: Synergistics, Inc.

Shumpeter, J. (2012) *The Theory of Economic Development.* Cambridge, MA: Harvard University Press.

Stela, D. (2013). Business globalization: Transnational corporations and global competition.

Studia Universitatis "Vasile Goldis" Arad. Seria Stiinte Economice, 23(2), 108–119.

Sustainable Brands. (2018, January 26). Trending: New Tools, Rules, Partnerships Take Food Waste, Hunger Head On. Retrieved February 02, 2018, from http://www.sustainablebrands.com/news_and_views/waste_not/sustainable_brands/trending_new_tools_rules_partnerships_take_food_waste_hu

Thomley, B., Wood, D., Grace, K., & Sarah, S. (2011). Impact investing: A framework for policy design and analysis. *Pacific Community*, 104. Retrieved from http://www.rockefellerfoundation.org/uploads/files/88fdd93f-b778-461e-828c-5c526ffed184-impact.pdf

Zupan, M.A. (2011). The Virtues of Free Markets. Cato Journal, *31*(2), 171–198. Retrieved from http://ezproxy.liberty.edu/login?url=https://search.proquest.com/docview/875294414?accountid=12085

PART 2:

Practice of Social
Entrepreneurship

Learning Outcomes

- Provide examples of different models of social enterprise
- Consider the methods of identifying a social problem
- Explain the different between integrated and differentiated models
- Analyze each aspect of a successful business model

Key Terms

Business Model	Integrated Hybrid
Calling	Model of Change
Demand	Opportunity Recognition
Differentiated Hybrid	Revenue
Effective Altruism	Value Proposition

Models and Opportunity Recognition

Introduction

In building upon the content provided in Chapter 1 regarding the definition of social entrepreneurship, we will now look at some of the models that are used to understand how social enterprises are established and structured. When looking at business models, we can also see a lot of overlap between conventional and social enterprises. This chapter will see strong similarities in the way that opportunity recognition occurs, as well as the manner in which a sustainable business model is developed. The questions that are asked of each organization regarding value propositions and revenue will be similar regardless of whether the enterprise has a core social mission or not. This is helpful as social entrepreneurs can use existing models and frameworks in new and innovative ways.

Business Model

The plan the business has to convert resources to meet market demand for a product or service while taking into account costs and revenue.

Opportunity Recognition

The identification of a use for a method or model to solve an existing problem.

Revenue

The inflow of financial returns to a company.

Status Quo

When we look at so many social problems and challenges that persist in societies, in spite of cultural and technological advances—such as greater access to education, along with so many other new and exciting developments globally—it can be hard to understand how these social, cultural, and human needs can still go unfulfilled.

What is it about the current situation that allows needs and challenges to go unmet and unresolved? What is it about the status quo and the current state of the culture, society, economy, or government that allows a social concern or problem to go unmet or unaddressed?

What we can see is that so many of the challenges that are faced in social situations are a result of competing interests, unrealized potential, or structures that have been allowed to persist in spite of their ineffectiveness. The social entrepreneur has to be willing to question the status quo and challenge existing paradigms of thought, action, and activities in order to be able to understand why the limitations exist. These questions can be tough, and people may not like the answers they find. These questions include, Who benefits from this problem persisting? Who stands to lose from solving the problem? Whose interests are at stake in the problem? This harkens back to Stakeholder Theory, which we discussed earlier in the book. It does take a level of personal courage and conviction and a willingness to see outside of the existing paradigm, or to challenge existing norms, in order to ask these types of questions.

As we look at the opportunity recognition and the way in which change occurs, it is helpful for us to begin to look at models of transformation and how information and questions can be changed into actionable concrete solutions.

Model of Change

Model of Change

A description the factors that are a part of transformation processes.

Understanding social entrepreneurship, and entrepreneurship in general, requires an understanding about the forces and factors that lead to change. Martin and Osberg (2015) provide four stages of transformation that can help gain a better understanding about how change occurs. Each one of these provides a broad understanding of what it takes to move change and to engage forces in a transformative process. Martin and Osberg describe the stages as

1. Understanding the world
2. Envisioning a new future
3. Building a model for change
4. Scaling the solution

A key component in entrepreneurial endeavors is the ability to recognize opportunity. This is true whether it is a social enterprise or a conventional enterprise. The ability to see a need and develop a new or innovative method of meeting that need drives the entrepreneurial process. In looking at the four stages of transformation, the opportunity recognition is the driving force to move a system or a social structure from one equilibrium to the next.

Problem Identification

Opportunity recognition for the social and the conventional entrepreneur have similar qualities, and the models can look alike. In this section we will look at some of the ways a social entrepreneur can recognize a problem and work to develop a possible business model to provide the solution. There are no real shortcuts, and it is this type of activity that can determine the long-term viability of the endeavor. It is also where an individual can go off course. If they do not take the time to engage in the rigorous up-front research into the problem, they may waste money and time in ineffective activities.

Effective Altruism

In an effort to help individuals sift through the variety of problems that they may see in the world, the Center for Effective Altruism (CEA) at Oxford provides an outline that individuals can use to help determine whether or not they should pursue a solution to a particular social need. (https://80000hours.org/career-guide/most-pressing-problems/)

> **Effective Altruism**
>
> Activity engaged in for the good of others in a systematic and measurable way.

The CEA lists out the following questions to help a social entrepreneur hone in on a specific area to address. While this is not a universal model, it can be helpful for the individual who feels a bit overwhelmed by the number of problems that exist, and is not sure where to start.

1. Is the problem large in scale?
   This question wants the individual to determine if the problem is widespread or if it is highly localized. We must be willing to look past our intuition and not assume that because we think there is a problem that there is sufficient data to support that conclusion. By looking objectively at the data surrounding a problem we can see if our perception of a widespread issue is, in fact, a large-scale issue. The scale matters because, as one begins to address the issue, even a 1% change in a very large problem represents a larger positive social benefit.

2. Is the problem neglected?
   This aspect of opportunity recognition has the individual seek out a problem for which there is a high likelihood of disproportionate positive returns. This asks the social entrepreneur to seek out the "low hanging fruit" as these types of activities can have a large impact proportional to the effort placed in them. Conversely, there are diminishing returns for the activities for which a large amount of previous effort has been employed. For example, there are a large number of resources being devoted to the eradication of breast cancer, and while an individual contribution will have an impact, that impact may be small. On the other hand, investment in a neglected problem, such as the need for mosquito nets in remote areas of the world that suffer from malaria, may have a disproportionately large impact. (Gordon, 2016).

3. Is the problem solvable?

   The third question requires the individual to determine if the problem they are looking to address is solvable in an effective way. There are numerous social programs that are not perceived as quantifiably effective, and are not actually solving the problem (Borzaga & Defourny, 2001; Kerlin, 2006). This is an important question because it gets to the heart of effective altruism, which is meant to take a serious look at the effectiveness of social enterprises and programs.

Seeing a Problem

The first step to understanding how to find and recognize opportunities for social entrepreneurship and social innovation is that, for innovation to take place, an individual needs to be inquisitive. It starts off with a desire in an individual to know what is going on in the world around them, as well as the experiences of other people. When learning what is going on in the environment, or the sphere of experiences we have, we need to seek to understand why a situation exists and the underlying causes for the problem.

For example, we may look at a particular article or speak to someone who describes a social problem that appears to be widespread, such as poverty or particular type of disease or homelessness or a psychological condition, and come across information we didn't previously have access to or understand regarding a challenge that affects other people. The Internet and social media have also, as discussed in previous chapters, provided an unprecedented amount of information related to social problems and issues. An individual who has an interest in a particular type of social problem can find others from all over the world who have similar convictions. This allows for the sharing of information and solutions in a way that has never before been possible in all of human history. It can be daunting to be exposed to, and bear the emotional burden of, such a high number of social issues. How is a social entrepreneur able to sift through and find the issue that most inspires them to create change?

It is at this point where the values that we discussed in previous chapters come into play. What is seen as a problem for one individual might not be seen as a problem for another individual and vice versa, and this can be a useful and functional dynamic. Two individuals can look at the same problem but view it differently. One individual might be inclined to say that there is nothing that can be done, it is merely a matter of coming to terms with the way the world works, and the problem is neither desirable nor practical. However, another individual can look at the problem and believe that a solution is both desirable and possible. The values and the mindset of the individual entrepreneur are key to beginning to understand opportunity recognition.

It is therefore a characteristic of social entrepreneurs that they have the conviction to seek out a solution and the hope that the solution is possible. In that respect, the social entrepreneur does exercise a certain amount of faith that there is a solution and a way forward, even if none may be immediately evident. Different individuals may feel a stronger or more urgent pull or calling to address particular problems.

Calling

The compulsion that an individual feels in pursuing a particular activity.

If an individual has a personal experience with a problem, such as a relative who has dealt with discrimination due to a disability, they may have a stronger emotional connection and a stronger desire to solve that particular problem than a problem like the environment or another social issue. It is up to each individual to understand and follow the issues that most inspire them to action, and utilize that inspiration as fuel for their entrepreneurial activity. So as we can see, the ability to see a problem can be highly individualized, and each entrepreneur should have the space and freedom to pursue the issues they feel strongly about.

This is true of the conventional entrepreneur as well. They may see a particular unmet consumer need or new method or technology that has yet to be applied to a consumer experience in a certain way, and it may prompt them to begin to look for new

> **Demand**
>
> A desire or need for a service or product.

and innovative ways to deliver products or services to consumers. If we were to describe social issues as a type of demand a social entrepreneur is seeking to meet, we can begin to potentially draw some deeper correlations between conventional and social entrepreneurs.

Why Is There a Problem?

The ability to see a problem is the first step. The next step is to ask why the problem exists. In this idea generation phase, the social entrepreneur and the conventional entrepreneur are engaged in idea generation that can take the form of research, interviews, or information collection related to the particular circumstances or variables led to the problem. This is considered a research and information-gathering phase. It may involve interviews or researching statistical data or journal articles or even experts in the field.

Seemingly simple issues, when viewed in a more deliberate way, can become complex and multifaceted. It is also important in this phase that the entrepreneur be as objective as possible and seek all sides that may claim to understand the true nature of the problem. This requires humility and objective assessment, keeping in mind that the ultimate goal is to look for a solution, not to assign blame to particular person or system, as this may prove to ultimately be counterproductive. Because you never know where the solution may come from, or who may be involved in solving the problem, it is best to have as many allies as possible.

Research and information gathering is not glamorous, but it is vital. This is an important phase of entrepreneurship, as the social entrepreneur must understand why a particular problem exists, and all of the various factors that relate to that problem, so that a viable solution can be presented. The social entrepreneur is able to see a way past the current system and equilibrium to embrace a potentially new paradigm (Martin & Osberg, 2015). While change can be incremental, it can also be revolutionary. These revolutionary ideas may initially be rejected as unrealistic or too fantastic, but the social entrepreneur is willing to try to find a new way forward.

This research and information gathering, for the social entrepreneur, is comparable to the market research that a conventional entrepreneur would engage in to determine the nature of the unmet need. What is the demand, what is driving this particular problem, and what are the potential options available to meet the demand? Focus groups, research reports, the previous work of different agencies, all of these can come into play when looking at and addressing why a particular problem exists, and the specific factors that have led to it.

Understanding how different variables impact one particular issue is also important. While there may be particular characteristics that may correlate with a social problem, they may not necessarily cause the social problem. Discerning the difference between correlation and causation is key, as we begin to look at how to impact change. In this way, we can have confidence that the solution to a problem will not just hopefully affect change, but will likely or even probably affect change. This is an important note for both the social and the conventional entrepreneur. As the entrepreneurial mentality is not opposed to risk, it is not wise for an entrepreneur to engage in unnecessary risk. If the information can be known it should be collected and factored in to the return on investment. There are many unknowns, but every effort should be made to gather all the relevant information that is available and bring it to bear on the potential solutions to the problem.

Mauro Seed Company

©amenic181/Shutterstock.com

Mauro Seed Company is a privately held, family run company that sells non-GMO heirloom garden seed. The company was founded with a mission to reduce the effects of hunger around the world by empowering people to feed themselves. To accomplish this, they have adopted the buy-one, give-one model by donating one pack of seeds for every pack of seeds sold. In 2016 they donated enough seed to produce one million pounds of food for people in the US and around the world, and they have doubled that amount in 2017. They have also been featured in *Forbes* and the *Tennessean*, and have received an award from *USA Today* honoring organizations that give back.

After years of working for large software companies, Mauro Seed Company founder David Mauro decided he wanted to do something to give back to society. While volunteering at local food banks, he became frustrated from seeing the same people come in and out every week. He wanted to do something that provided a way for people to access a sustainable source of food and not rely as heavily on charitable aid from these food banks and similar organizations. Through his research, David found that distributing seed is the most efficient way to do this in terms of cost and scale. Having never worked in the food industry before, the business of selling seed was very new to David when he founded Mauro Seed Company in 2015. However, that did not stop him from pursuing his passion to end world hunger. David stated that, as he gains experience in the business, he continually learns how to improve his organization and find better ways to impact the lives of the people touched by Mauro Seed Company's products.

Who Is Able to Solve the Problem?

We may tend to think of entrepreneurs and innovators as those individuals who are unique and so special that we are unable to imagine ourselves in that way. The personas of Steve Jobs, Bill Gates, or Muhammad Yunus may seem so far removed from our own experience and our own abilities. Nevertheless, it is important for all individuals to realize that they have unique gifts and talents. Additionally, it can be daunting to be faced with the scope of a problem. When we look at the scope of homelessness or the effects of mental disability and psychological challenges in our society and indeed in the world, it can seem like too big of a problem to solve. An individual may be tempted to think, "I can't solve the entire problem, so why even try?" This type of thinking can lead to inaction and frustration for the individual who sees the problem.

Each individual who feels the deep pull to try to solve a social problem in an entrepreneurial way should use that pull to make an impact in whatever way possible. No individual can foresee the long-term ramifications of their actions. Even the smallest, and most seemingly insignificant act to try to make the lives of others better, can have long-term impacts. We should not let the potential for failure or seemingly insurmountable problems keep us from making the impact we can make. There are individuals who have been given the gifts and talents for certain activities.

Many of these gifts and talents are not the result of personal endeavors, although many are, and many are honed through effort. We can also look at those areas of our lives for which we feel naturally gifted. The question is, are we going to use these natural gifts to serve ourselves, or can we use these gifts to make the world around us better? Every person, no matter how seemingly insignificant the gift and talent, can use those gifts and talents make the world better. Social entrepreneurs can come from anywhere, and they can be anyone. If you feel called to help solve a social problem through entrepreneurial endeavors, that is all the qualification you need.

It may also be that the best chance to solve the problem is not an individual, but a form of government engagement or policy. There might be a particular policy that should be adjusted, or new legislation that may need to be drafted, to have the desired effect. Government is an option for some, but its impacts and limitations should be taken into account when assessing the situation. Again, Martin and Osberg provide a good understanding of the difference between government and individual action. Government action can tend to be broad in scope and benefit a great number of people. However, the mandatory and ubiquitous nature of the government program prevents it from potentially finding the best solution for the unique nature of some problems. Government intervention can tend to be a blunt object for change when a more nuanced and specialized business solutions might be more effective and efficient (Martin and Osberg, p. 56).

Solving the Problem

Seeing a problem and gaining the confidence to move forward toward a solution are the first two steps. However, ideas need concrete action and effective planning. In this phase, the social entrepreneur—and the conventional entrepreneur, for that matter—generate ideas, research, conduct interviews, and collect information related to why a problem exists.

Coupled with the ability to see a problem or social issue is the solving of that problem. This solution will likely be innovative. However, the term innovation should not cause unnecessary anxiety. We tend to think of innovation as being a creation *ex nihilo*, or out of nothing, but the reality is that innovation is the result of incremental small adjustments to existing processes or models. Schumpeter (2012) Has identified five types of innovation that are typically associated with entrepreneurial activity, or ways in which innovation can occur.

- Create a new or improved product.
- Create a new or improved strategy or method of operating.
- Reach a new market, or an unmet need.
- Use a new source, supply, or labor.
- Establish a new industrial or organizational structure.

Additionally, Dees (2001, *Toolkit for SE*) amended the list from Schumpeter with two more items, which he described as:

- Establish new terms of engagement, such as an unconditional satisfaction guarantee.
- Develop new funding structures.

Innovation can be incremental, and it does not need to be a large-scale disruption to an entire industry. Innovation can be a small change to an existing organization, or it can be applying an old technology in a new way. There are opportunities for different industries to begin to operate in more effective ways by simply working together. For example, the healthcare field is a part of innovation when they use existing data collection and analysis tools in a way that they haven't before. These tools existed, but they were not previously applied to this industry.

DC Central Kitchen

DC Central Kitchen is a community kitchen founded in 1989 in Washington, DC, that seeks to end the cycle of hunger and poverty in their community. They provide fourteen-week job training programs to people who have histories of incarceration, homelessness, addiction, and trauma so they can start culinary careers. These programs cost nothing to the students and 90% of graduates find employment after exiting the program. Many of the graduates are hired by DC Central Kitchen to prepare donated food for distribution to different nonprofits, schools, and homeless shelters. They produce more than three million meals every year. Founder Robert Egger developed this model because he believes that combating hunger by just giving food to the hungry does not address the root of the problem. While organizations that do this are a piece of solving the issue, they do not provide a long-term solution. However, by providing an opportunity for steady employment, they give the people the ability to provide for themselves. This addresses the source of widespread hunger: poverty.

DC Central Kitchen also helps reduce the amount of produce that is wasted at local farms. Much of the food grown on these farms is thrown out due to imperfections, even though there is nothing nutritionally wrong with it. DCCK purchases this produce for a fraction of the wholesale value to use in their kitchens. This is beneficial to both parties, because farmers receive revenue they would not have otherwise, and DCCK is able to receive much of their produce at a reduced price.

©Tyler Olson/Shutterstock.com

Another program DCCK started, Healthy Corners, addresses the issue of "food deserts," or areas that do not have access to fresh fruit, vegetables, and other healthful whole foods. Through this program, DCCK provides glass display refrigerators for produce to corner stores in the city. Initially, they provide the produce for free, but slowly they start to charge a fee. This allows the store owner to develop a market with little to no risk. DCCK has implemented this program in seventy-four stores, and other cities are starting to develop programs using the same model.

https://www.uschamberfoundation.org/food-data-great-opportunities
https://www.nationalgeographic.com/environment/urban-expeditions/food/dc-central-kitchen-food-interview/

After discussing some of the models of change and how opportunity recognition begins, we can turn our attention to moving the opportunity and solution into an actionable business model. The following sections will discuss the concept of business model and what it may look like for a social enterprise.

Organizational Structure and Models

A business model is driven by the method selected by the social entrepreneur to address the problem and to move forward in a sustainable way. The business model brings together the various factors of supply, demand, product, logistics, distribution, and personnel in a cohesive and effective way. Each part of the business model, and each step of the logistics chain, should be consistent and in keeping with the overall financial goals and mission of the company.

As we begin to put forth potential models, it is important to keep in mind the need for the model to match the mission and not the other way around. The model should match the identified problem, solution, and outcome in the most effective and sustainable way. In every aspect of the business the entrepreneur should ensure they are engaging in value-added transactions, as this helps to ensure long-term viability and success.

Osterwalder and Pigneur (2010) have provided a helpful map for thinking about business models and the relationships that exist between the various aspects related to business operation.

KEY PARTNERS	KEY ACTIVITIES	VALUE PROPOSITION	AUDIENCE RELATIONSHIPS	AUDIENCE SEGMENTS
Who will help you? • Who are your key partners/suppliers? • What are the most important motivations for the partnerships?	**How do you do it?** • What key activities does your value proposition require? • What activities are most important for your distribution channels, customer relationships, revenue streams, etc.?	**Who do you do?** • What core value do you deliver to your audience? • Which needs are you satisfying?	**How do you interact?** • What relationship does the target audience expect you to establish? • How can you integrate that into your work in terms of cost and format?	**Who do you help?** • Which groups are you creating value for? • Who is your most important audience?

DISTRIBUTION CHANNELS

How do you reach them?
• Through which channel does your audience want to be reached?
• Which channels work best? How much do they cost?
• How can they be integrated into your and your audiences routines?

KEY RESOURCES

What do you need?
• What key resources does your value proposition require?

COST STRUCTURE	REVENUE STREAM
What will it cost? • What are the most important costs in your work? • Which key resources/activities are most expensive?	**How much will you make?** • For what value are your audiences willing to pay? • What and how do they recently pay? How would they prefer to pay? • How much does every revenue stream contribute to the overall revenues?

Figure 4.1 Business model canvas

© Kendall Hunt Publishing Company. Used with permission.

54 **Introduction to Social Entrepreneurship**

At the core of what drives the model is determining what need is being met. Everything else is meant to support the existence of that value proposition (Nesta, 2014). Along with the value proposition, Osterwalder and Pigneur (2010) list the following aspects of business model.

1. Key partners
2. Key activities
3. Key resources
4. Audience relationships
5. Distribution channels
6. Audience segments
7. Cost structure
8. Revenue stream

We will first take a look at the value proposition. When we look at who the customer or end user is for a social enterprise, it may look differently based on the unique mission and model of each organization. For example, if the social good is created exclusively through the exchange of a good or service that is targeted at a specific social group, then that is the primary customer or audience for the business. However, if there are customers who purchase goods or services, and then the profit or revenue from that exchange is then given to another target audience, then the business model should show and reflect the value proposition for each group.

> **Value Proposition**
>
> The physical and nonphysical items that are provided to another in a market-based exchange that an individual deems to be important.

Once we turn the key value proposition for the intended audience and target market, we can ask the next following questions which are, how will we obtain the value proposition or meet the value proposition (What are the key activities?), and what resources do we need to meet those activities (What are the key resources?). The key activities and the key resources allow the business model define what activities are most important for the value proposition. For example, if the value proposition requires the education of particular segments of society, then education programs and activities related to that, and teachers and classrooms, will be key resources. Following the activities and resources are the partners and suppliers of these activities and resources. For example, who will the teachers be and where will you find them to hire them?

From this point on we can also look at the cost structure (What will it cost?). The key activities, resources, and partners should all factor into the cost structure. Costs are those items associated with helping to provide the key partners with the resources to accomplish activities.

Also, for understanding how we will meet the value proposition of what we do, we will we look at the distribution channels (How do you interact?) and audience relationships (How do you reach them?). These two questions will depend on the audience as there may be distribution channels that include intermediaries such as stores or retail outlets, while others may have a distribution channel that goes directly to the audience and the user. Again, as discussed earlier, the distribution channel for the customer and the distribution channel for the beneficiary may be different depending on the method and model for each organization. This is reflected in the audience segments aspect of the business model canvas. For which groups are you creating value? It is also from this side of the business model canvas that we can see the inclusion of the revenue stream (How much will you make?). It is this aspect of the model where discussions regarding how much a particular item should cost, the method of payment, and weather all the audience or market segments pay the same amount.

Hybrid Organization

When we discuss a hybrid organization we are talking about an enterprise that blends together both revenue generating activities as well as social activities, basically our definition of social enterprise. Social enterprises and the models used by social entrepreneurs can be categorized into two types, integrated and differentiated hybrids (Battilana, Lee, Walker, & Dorsey, 2012).

Integrated Hybrid

A type of organization in which the beneficiaries of social value and the customers or consumers of the product or service are the same individuals.

The integrated hybrid is described as a type of organization in which the beneficiaries of social value and the customers or consumers of the product or service are the same individuals. For example, when we think about an educational institution that specifically serves underprivileged individuals at a reduced cost, the beneficiaries and the consumers are integrated into the same audience.

Differentiated Hybrid

Whenever the consumers or audience of the commercial activities are separate from the audience that is the recipient of the social benefit and value.

The differentiated hybrid is whenever the consumers or audience of the commercial activities are separate from the audience that is the recipient of the social benefit and value. For example, an organization that sells coffee and then uses the revenue from the coffee sales to fund safe houses for women in developing countries would be a differentiated hybrid.

The challenge for the differentiated hybrid organization is how to maintain fidelity to the financial as well as social goals of the organization. It is important to understand the relationship, and difference, between consumers and the beneficiaries of the social enterprise.

Competitive Advantage

An effective model includes, and sufficiently answers, all the questions described in the business model canvas. It will help the social entrepreneur determine whether the business plan or model is viable if, after accounting for all of the value propositions, resources, and activities associated with providing the value proposition, the organization is still able to maintain enough resources to continue to operate. However, businesses do not operate in a closed economic system, and other organizations might soon establish similar models and begin to operate in ways that jeopardize the long-term viability of the organization.

It is at this point that we must discuss the idea of competitive advantage. Every box surrounding the value proposition is an opportunity for a social enterprise to establish a competitive advantage. Competitive advantage is when a business has an advantage over other businesses that might operate in the same market, which is extremely difficult or perhaps highly unlikely to be duplicated by another organization. For example, an organization might have an exclusive contractual arrangement with a key supplier of a resource needed in the value proposition. That exclusive relationship prevents other businesses and organizations from offering the same product or service at the same price. Additionally, there might be exclusive access to a target audience granted by a prearranged agreement with a civic organization that prevents other organizations from operating in the same space. Each one of these might be considered a competitive advantage for a social enterprise. Every aspect of the business model canvas should seek competitive advantage over other firms. The more of an advantage that a social enterprise has over the competition, the greater likelihood for long-term viability.

The concept of competition and competitive advantage provides a unique challenge for the social enterprise. In the typical business endeavor the goal is for the business to grow and develop by meeting demand better than other organizations or businesses. This means that if there is limited market share, the growth of one company will come at the expense of another company. This type of competition forces organizations to adjust and change to continually meet consumer demands better than the competitor in order to exist. However, in the social enterprise space, it might present unique and potentially ethical challenges for the social entrepreneur. For example, if two organizations are both seeking the same social outcome and social value proposition to the same population or target audience, do they have an obligation to work together to accomplish the greater social good, or should one business seek to grow and develop at the expense of the other business? The latter may jeopardize the current social value created by the other social enterprise.

We may see types of this that exist right now in the nonprofit space, with organizations "competing" for some of the same donors or limited philanthropic funds or grants. However, as more social enterprises develop and begin, there may be more issues related to the moral and social ramifications of competition between social enterprises that occur.

Tax Status

You might have noticed that so far in this chapter we haven't looked at whether or not a social enterprise should be a nonprofit or a for-profit organization. This is by design, as the chosen tax status of the organization will be a function of the model and the value proposition. Determining which tax status is most appropriate for the organization is important, but the tax status should serve the value proposition not the other way around. There are pros and cons to each option. In the following chapter we will look at these distinctions and how each one might best serve the model.

Conclusion

In this chapter we began by looking at the way in which social enterprises and entrepreneurial endeavors begin. By first understanding the forces and factors that bring about change we were able to look at the beginning of any entrepreneurial endeavor which is opportunity recognition. However, recognizing an opportunity is only the first step in effectively bringing about substantive long-term change to a problem. We looked at how to move a recognition into an actionable business model. The next chapter will focus on the ways in which for-profit and nonprofit organizations are organized and how each one can be used effectively in a social enterprise model.

References

Battilana, J., Lee, M., Walker, J., & Dorsey, C. (2012, Summer). In search of the hybrid ideal. *Stanford Social Innovation Review, 10*, 51–55. Retrieved from http://ezproxy.liberty.edu/login?url=https://search.proquest.com/docview/1018738257?accountid=12085

Borzaga, C., & Defourny, J. (2001). Conclusions: Social enterprises in Europe: A diversity of initiatives and prospects. In C. Borzaga & J. Defourny (Eds.), The Emergence of Social Enterprise (pp. 350–370). London, New York: Routledge.

Dees, J. G. (2001). The meaning of social entrepreneurship. *Spotlight*, 1–16. https://doi.org/10.1108/14626000710773529

Gordon, M. (2016). How social enterprises change: The perspective of the evolution of technology. *Journal of Social Entrepreneurship, 0676*(January). https://doi.org/10.1080/19420676.2015.1086410

Kerlin, J. A. (2006). Social enterprise in the United States and Europe: Understanding and learning from the differences. *Voluntas: International Journal of Voluntary and Nonprofit Organizations, 17*(3), 247–263. https://doi.org/10.1007/s11266-006-9016-2

Nesta. (2014). Development Impact & You: Practical Tools to trigger and Support Social Innovation. Retrieved from http://diytoolkit.org/media/DIY-Toolkit-Full-Download-A4-Size.pdf

Osterwalder, A., Pigneur, Y. (2010) Business Model Generation. Available online from www.businessmodelgeneration.com

Roger L. Martin & Sally R. Osberg. **Getting Beyond Better: How Social Entrepreneurship Works** 248 pages, Harvard Business Review Press, 2015.

Shumpeter, J. (2012). *The Theory of Economic Development*. Cambridge, MA: Harvard University Press.

The Center for Effective Altruism (CEA) Which global problem is most important to work on? What the evidence says. (2017). Retrieved February 10, 2018, from https://80000hours.org/career-guide/most-pressing-problems/

Chapter 5

Structures

Learning Outcomes

- Recognize some of the legal entities used to form social enterprises
- Summarize the difference between various business structures
- Assess the dangers of mission drift
- Outline the primary considerations of organizational structures

Key Terms

Benefit Corporation
Community Contribution Corporation
Community Foundation
Community Interest Corporation

Cooperatives
L3C
Private Ownership

Introduction

In the previous chapter we looked at models of change and models of business. These models focused primarily on an organization's costs, revenue, and audience. However, there are many organizational models available that are geared toward social progress and development. As the growth and development of social enterprises becomes more common, the limitations of nonprofit and for-profit distinctions are proving insufficient to meet the demands of new social entrepreneurs.

These business model distinctions are a result of the ways in which governments have worked to develop, and ultimately encourage, legal and taxable structures specifically devoted to social good and market orientation.

The following discussion of organizational structures and models is not meant to be exhaustive or to show all of the possible types of legal structures around the world. It is instead meant to provide a current snapshot of the ways governments and political oversight agencies are beginning to recognize and establish formal structures beyond the traditional nonprofit and for-profit models. As the growth of social enterprise endeavors grows, it is appropriate for there to be an even greater degree of diversity in a list such as this. Additionally, these descriptions should not serve as any form of legal or accounting advice; they are for informational purposes only. Professional counsel is necessary and recommended for any legal company formation.

Limitations of Traditional Structures

The typical distinction that is made, at least here in the United States, between those organizations that exist for social benefit versus those that operate with a goal of personal financial gain for the owners, is made by a distinction in which the organizations are taxed and governed. The for-profit company is a great vehicle for the traditional owner who wants to maximize the return on investment for the company. The ability to make a profit is a motivating factor for most business owners, and the for-profit structure allows that to become a reality if the owner is able to create enough revenue from the sale of goods or services to outpace the costs of running the business. It also allows the owner to seek out investors for the company. These investors can purchase a part of the company in return for a share of the company's profits. The owners of the business then pay taxes on the profits they generate and obtain through the company. There are no limits on the amount of profit a company can make. Even with investors, the owners can continue to operate as the sole decision makers for the company vision, mission, and strategy.

However, a for-profit company can have some challenges if they are seeking to work toward the establishment of a social mission alongside profit maximization. One of the main challenges is the dynamic that exists with their investors. The individuals who invest in a company do so with the understanding that the directors will engage in activities that will maximize the financial return on their investment. The managers for the for-profit company have a fiduciary responsibility to the investors to act in ways that will help to ensure that the financial return of their investment is maximized. This dynamic may put the interests of social good at odds with the financial return of owners and investors. A manager may not engage in activity that intentionally reduces profits for a social good if the investors are expecting the highest financial return possible.

Additionally, there are limits on the information that a for-profit company must disclose to the public related to the ways in which funds are spent in the business operations. This level of privacy makes it a challenge for those investors who may be interested in socially conscious business activities to know that the managers are working toward a truly double bottom line. The for-profit company is fairly predictable. The producers and consumers agree on a price for goods and services and engage in a mutually beneficial transaction.

The nonprofit company is traditionally set up as a way for an organization to establish a structure that shows they place a higher priority on social impact over profits. It does not mean that they will not make profits, but that the profits and business interactions have limits. For example, there are no options for investors in nonprofits. Funds from external sources, that are not a result of an exchange, are considered donations, which is incentivized with a tax benefit for the donor.

Additionally, the nonprofit company has a board of directors that oversees the company and helps guide the director of the company toward agreed-upon social goals. This is an extra layer of accountability for the company, and it helps to keep the mission at the forefront of the company activities.

The challenge for the nonprofit company is that any profits cannot be distributed to the board or the managers, which can serve as a disincentive for the managers to engage in activities that maximize financial income. Additionally, since there can be no investors, there is a challenge when trying to reach out to traditional sources for capital and funding. The nonprofit organization must rely on the donations of others as well as the sales of any goods or services provided by the company. This dynamic places a high value on the ability of the board and director to be effective at fundraising. Fundraising activities can be a financial burden to the organization, and the director and board may spend an inordinate amount of time raising money instead of working to establish more effective and efficient strategies for the nonprofit to manage their social mission and goals.

Organizational Structures for Social Enterprises

In an effort to establish creative ways for organizations to work toward a balance between profits and social outcomes, some countries have established a variety of new officially recognized business licenses. The following sections will describe some of the ways in which organizations are being developed to help bring together the strengths of both nonprofits and for-profits in order to bring about positive social benefit and to encourage social entrepreneurship.

Private Ownership

TOMS (primarily known for shoes) is an example of a privately owned social enterprise. The company was started by an entrepreneur who self-funded the startup of the company, which pursued the following model: for each pair of shoes purchased, the company donates one pair of shoes to an individual in an impoverished part of the world.

Because TOMS was able to begin with financing from the individual owner, the company did not have to raise a lot of capital from investors to cover start-up costs. This company was able to maintain profitability in alignment with its social mission, so it is a great example of social enterprise, and the founder is a good example of a successful social entrepreneur (Reiser, 2012). Typical social entrepreneurs may not have the capital to begin a company and incur some of associated the start-up costs, but this method is an option available to social entrepreneurs. The owner of TOMs eventually sold part of the company to an investment firm for a large sum, and only time will tell whether the company is able to maintain the balance between profits and social goals.

Warby Parker is another example of a privately owned company that has a dual mission of social goals and profits (Reiser, 2012). Warby Parker has a "buy one, give one" model similar to TOMS (Fitzgerald, 2015). However, Warby Parker has also added an extra dimension, by donating cash from the sale of glasses to VisionSpring. VisionSpring is a nonprofit that trains locals in developing countries to sell glasses at low prices (https://www.entrepreneur.com/article/242437).

Nonprofit

Nonprofit companies, and not-for-profit companies, which are incorporated under IRS code 501(c) in the United States (Government Publishing Office), are not subject to federal income tax. Nonprofits are companies that are governed by a board of directors and run by appointed executives. Nonprofits can benefit from donations that are tax deductible and are able to engage in fundraising efforts to encourage such donations. Nonprofits and not-for-profits are not exactly the same, but we will use them interchangeably in this discussion, and focus on the similarities.

A nonprofit is unable to distribute any excess revenue, as there are no shareholders or owners of the company. Nonprofits can enter into contracts as well as own assets. The nonprofit company is typically associated with volunteer and charitable organizations, but it does not prohibit the company from producing revenue or profits.

For example, Goodwill Industries International, Inc. is able to take donated items at their stores and then sell those items to the public at low cost (Goodwill, 2018). This model allows the individuals providing the donations to earn a tax benefit, while allowing Goodwill to generate revenue and provide low-cost clothing and other items to those with limited incomes.

Nonprofits have the opportunity to raise revenue and financing through the tax incentive benefits of donations. Additionally, they are able to apply for grants and other sources of funding to help offset operating costs.

Community Foundation

Community Foundation
A publicly supported charity that exists as a vehicle for communities to set up trusts that are directed toward activities, specifically related to improving the community in which it operates.

The **Community Foundation** is a publicly supported charity that exists as a vehicle for communities to set up trusts directed toward activities specifically related to improving the community in which each branch operates (Johnson & Jones, 1994). The first Community Foundation was set up in Cleveland, Ohio in 1914, and has since then grown to the point where there are hundreds in the United States, and hundreds more abroad, with a growing number of community foundations in the UK (Daly, 2008).

The goal of the Community Foundation is to create a tax friendly way for communities to establish philanthropic foundations in their community with the goal of meeting community-specific needs. It is focused on a specific geographic area and the recipients of the resources are intended to be within that area (Council on Foundations). The Community Foundation is not specifically a social enterprise, as we have defined it in this book, but it is an attempt by civic organizations to bridge the gap between private philanthropy and government activity.

The funds in a Community Foundation can be endowed or expendable, meaning that the funds can be used to accrue interest, and that interest continues the work of the fund, which makes it self-sufficient. Or the Community Foundation can be expendable, meaning that the fund can be completely used up and replenished by the donations of those who contribute.

There are a number of criteria that must be met for a Community Foundation to maintain its status as such (gpo.gov). The Community Foundation must have a common governing body, or a common distribution committee, which ensures that the distribution of funds is for charitable purposes and meets the needs of the community. This committee also ensures that the foundation is able to maintain the status of Community Foundation. It also helps ensure continued mission and purpose for the funds.

Since the Community Foundation relies on the donations of those within the community, there is a level of accountability and oversight that allows the funds to be quickly and effectively distributed to the programs or organizations that show the most opportunity for success. Additionally, because of the local focus of these foundations, the feedback regarding effectiveness can be quick and accurate.

The Community Foundation, while not specifically a social enterprise, does represent an opportunity for the social entrepreneur to understand the impact that local knowledge of a community, and the problems in that area can have on the ways in which communities organize and work together to solve those problems.

Benefit Corporation (Wilburn & Wilburn, 2014)

A benefit corporation is a for-profit company that has demonstrated a dual mission to making profits and promoting social good. In order for a company to exist as a legally registered benefit corporation, the company is required to create a benefit report. This status blends together state-approved legal status, but can also include certification by a third party.

> **Benefit Corporation (B Corp)**
>
> A for-profit company that has demonstrated a dual mission to making profits and promoting social good.

This third-party standard can come from organizations, such as B Lab or the Global Reporting Initiative, after the company shows that they have a commitment to company stakeholders in their forming documents. Upon obtaining certification from B Lab, the corporation can use the B Lab mark on their products. This mark then serves to communicate the social commitment that the company has made to the consumers of the product or service (Resier, 2011). The certification from the third-party organization does not confer legal status on the organization. However, it is a way for companies to display the depth of their commitment to stakeholders in a way that is easy for consumers and investors to see.

The legal status of a benefit corporation is registered and granted by the state in which the corporation operates. This status specifically requires that the goal of social value be a part of the articles of incorporation of the company. However, an existing company may be able to convert to a benefit corporation with a sufficient amount of shareholder support.

The benefit corporation must assess their social impact annually in a report, and, in the majority of states, make that information available to the general public (Reiser, 2011; Wilburn & Wilburn, 2014). This allows for the public to determine the impact of the benefit corporation on the social value to which they have committed. The benefit corporation status also protects the social goals of the company, should the ownership of the business change.

Community Contribution Corporation

The community contribution corporation, or CCC, is a business distinction that exists in Canada as an attempt by the Canadian government to develop a social enterprise distinction that is able to exist to meet the needs of the social entrepreneurs in the country. There are a few unique aspects of the CCC that are a part of what makes it socially beneficial. First, the CCC is a for-profit entity and is allowed to make decisions in pursuit of profits. However, the company has a cap on how much of the dividends can be distributed to the directors or shareholders. The cap for dividends is at 40%, and the resulting 60% of the dividends must be directed toward social and community goals (BC Ministry of Finance, 2017).

Additionally, there must be at least three directors for the company throughout the life of the company, as this adds an additional level of accountability to the company's mission and vision for the social good. The company must submit an annual community contribution report to the government in order to maintain the CCC classification.

This distinction is an effort on the part of the government in British Columbia to merge the strengths of traditional nonprofit and for-profit organizations. The ability to attract investors into a for-profit company while maintaining the social focus of a nonprofit organization is the goal of the CCC distinction. It also allows the company to take advantage of any branding benefits for consumers who are looking to engage with a business that is fundamentally devoted to social benefits and goals. An example of this kind of organization is Urban Matters, a CCC that assists individuals and communities in developing scalable solutions to social challenges (http://www.urbanmatters.ca/). The primary revenue driver for Urban Matters is offering consulting services to those organizations who wish to utilize their expertise.

Community Interest Company

The Community Interest Company (CIC) is a legal status that is available to companies in the United Kingdom through the Office of the Regulator of Community Interest Companies (ORCIC). The CIC can be of varying size. CIC status is conferred by the government on companies that intend to engage in trade for social purposes. There are few restrictions on what specific social purposes can be used. These companies are monitored by the ORCIC. One of the unique features of the CIC is that it is subject to an "asset lock," which means that there are restrictions on how the profits can be distributed to the shareholders as dividends. These locked assets must be used to further the stated social goals of the company. Additionally, the CIC may not transfer assets at less than market value, except to another asset-lock company or to the community. There is also a provision that requires the locked assets to be transferred to the community or to another asset-lock company in the event that the company dissolves.

The CIC must submit an annual report to the government regarding their use of the funds for both operations and social good, and this report is available to the public online for them to view (BIS Guidance).

Making these aspects of the company public is an effort by the government to make the CIC accountable to the government as well as the society in which the business operates. It is this public accountability that the government hopes will help deter organizations that may want to utilize the CIC distinction exclusively for marketing purposes. This also underscores the desire for companies to be seen as socially responsible and socially active. Ultimately, the CIC distinction will help provide a level of accountability along with strong social branding for companies that want to blend social and financial returns.

The CIC was established as a quick and easy way for a social enterprise to be established with very little specific guidance regarding what does and does not constitute a community benefit (Nicholls, 2010). This makes it easier for for-profit companies to go out and pitch viable ideas to investors with the opportunity for a return on their investment, with the understanding that the caps on these returns do exist. Additionally, it allows nonprofits to have the opportunity to raise capital from investors and limit voting or ownership rights.

The CIC status in the UK has had some challenges in the past, with not every CIC finding it possible to maintain the social and financial balance necessary to continue to operate (Macalister, 2008). However, others have been successful, and still others have had mixed results. Wellbeing Enterprises is an example of a CIC located in the UK that offers opportunities for community members to engage in wellness activities, including painting and techniques for mindfulness (http://www.wellbeingenterprises.org.uk/about/). This type of organization also seeks to recruit and help young social entrepreneurs establish their own social enterprises as a part of their services.

The CIC model represents a strong show of support from the government for social enterprises and is an attempt to develop a standardized model for such activities. While there may be some room for discussion regarding the nature of the asset lock and the limitations on distributions to the investors, time will determine whether or not this type of model has the potential to be an acceptable legislative approach for other countries. The Community Interest Company can be formatted in three ways: limited by guarantee, limited by shares, or a public limited company.

CIC: Limited by Guarantee

A report prepared for the City of London in 2013 (ICF GHK, 2013) showed that 69% of social venture companies were companies limited by guarantee (CLG). This corporate status describes a company that obtains funding from guarantors, but does not provide shares, since the guarantors are debt-based investors (Thomley, Wood, & Grace, 2011). The guarantors are given voting status in the company, with the amount of liability of the guarantors proportional to the amount they guarantee. However, the profits from the company are reinvested into the company or diverted to a charity. This option is attractive to social entrepreneurs, as it allows for external funding, but it can retain the not-for-profit status that allows it to also attract grants and public sector contracts.

CIC: Limited by Shares

A CIC that is limited by shares is an equity-based option for a CIC. The dividends paid to the shareholders of these CICs are capped as a percentage of the profits (Thomley, Wood, & Grace, 2011). Additionally, since the investors of a CIC limited by shares purchase partial ownership in the company, the more shares that someone owns, the more influence they have over the decision-making in the company.

Both the CIC that is limited by shares and the CIC that is limited by guarantee provide options for companies to be able to raise capital and finance their operations through the investment of funds from outside sources. This allows the organization to not have to finance all debt through loans, which have to be repaid at a rate that is typically higher than the dividends paid to investors. Additionally, it is a source of more permanent capital, as opposed to the temporary capital of a loan. However, since the shareholders are able to receive distributions from the profits, they are not able to benefit from grants. The investors are also able to go into the CIC knowing that a certain percentage of the funds will be used in the pursuit of the social goals of the company; this is a value added for the investor (Brown, 2006).

CAUSEGEAR L3C

CAUSEGEAR was founded as an L3C that uses 90% of its profits to benefit its employees. They employ men and women in India to manufacture high-quality fashion apparel. According to the 2016 Global Slavery Index, an estimated 45.8 million people, across 167 countries, are affected by a form of modern slavery. In India alone, there are estimated to be over 18 million people living in modern slavery, most of whom are women. It is CAUSEGEAR's mission to bring these men and women to freedom by attacking the main cause of slavery in the region, poverty. On average, a purchase of one item from CAUSEGEAR provides one day of freedom for their workers.

According to the World Bank, there are over 750 million people in the world living on less than $1.90 a day. CAUSEGEAR's L3C model allows them to operate in the most efficient way to make the most impact on the lives of their crafters. Currently, CAUSEGEAR is able to pay wages that are five times the average amount given to men and women currently working in the industry. They believe that giving people the opportunity to provide for themselves is the best way to end the cycle of unfathomable poverty, and as a result slavery, that affects much of the world today. This is because having steady jobs will reduce these people's dependency on charitable aid. CAUSEGEAR's founder Brad Jeffery believes charitable aid is a very temporary fix and does not address the underlying reasons for the existence of poverty. He also strongly believes that there needs to be a shift in the mind of the consumer to not fall into the seduction of big businesses that take advantage of these people affected by extreme poverty.

Low-Profit Limited Liability Company (L3C)

The low-profit limited liability company is a business distinction allowed by the US government whereby a company can add in different ownership structures for the members, with varying levels of decision making. For example, a company could transfer part ownership to a private foundation, which would help to provide a level of accountability to the social mission of the company (Ebrahim, Battilana, Mair, 2014).

> **Low-Profit Limited Liability Company (L3C)**
>
> A business distinction allowed by the government whereby a company can add in different ownership structures to the members, with varying levels of decision making.

The creation of the L3C status allows foundations and other social enterprises to enter into arrangements with a for-profit business, in a way that is in keeping with the program-related investments (PRI) required by law for such organizations, while opening them up for the potential for a return on the investment. Foundations are required to spend at least 5% of their assets per year in order to maintain their tax-exempt status (Brakman, Reiser, 2013). They typically do this through grants. However, the creation of the L3C organization allows a foundation to use that 5% PRI in a L3C company that has a specific social mission, thereby allowing the foundation to meet the PRI requirement, while opening up the opportunity for a return on that 5% investment (Witkins, 2009).

From an accountability and oversight perspective, however, the L3C has limitations. This is due to the fact that the L3C does not mandate a balance between the financial and social concerns, but merely allows the flexibility to allow for it. Again, this differs from other types of models, but it does indicate the variability of how different governments are working to try to open up the social enterprise sector to more of a blended system between for-profits and social value organizations.

The L3C relies on the oversight of the governing board to ensure the proper balance between social and financial returns, but there is no standardized metric to ensure that the appropriate balance is being met. Additionally, the L3C can convert to a for-profit traditional LLC if the directors of the company decide to no longer pursue the same adherence to the social mission.

> **Private Ownership**
>
> Ownership of property or assets by an individual or group of individuals, as opposed to a government or public entity.

This, in effect, transfers the money into private ownership and moves away from the social mission of the company all together.

Cooperatives

Is a worker cooperative (a cooperative owned and self-managed by its workers) a social entrepreneurial endeavor? Some argue that it does in fact fall under the umbrella of social enterprise. This is because, depending on the goal of the worker cooperative and its underlying purpose, a social issue can be mitigated with the presence of this cooperative. With the goal of a social enterprise being to bring social value to those impacted by their business, a worker cooperative is benefiting those who work for the business. For example, if an entrepreneur set up a worker cooperative in a low-income community, bettering the community through the cooperative's production of goods/services and even generating income for those who work at the cooperative, the cooperative will positively impact the community (Rothschild, 2009).

A social cause can change depending on the setting of the worker cooperative. For example, the social benefit of one cooperative in America was to provide jobs and work options to a particular immigrant community. In contrast, the social benefit of one cooperative in Argentina was to mitigate gender inequalities in the broader society by allowing equal membership voting rights within the worker cooperative. During a recession, one cooperative in Finland had the social goal of providing jobs for the unemployed.

Cooperatives

An enterprise that is owned and operated by the members of that organization.

Worker **cooperatives** focus strongly on meeting the needs of their workers and letting them have a voice in the company. The member-workers control the cooperatives. The traditional hierarchy of an organization is minimized because each member of the cooperative has a vote in the governance of the business. Each member has an equal voting right and elects members to be on the board of directors. They strongly focus on solidarity and the development of their communities.

Not only are the cooperatives worker controlled, but they are also worker owned and worker beneficial. This means that the workers share the profits among their worker-members, in contrast to for-profit company's shareholders splitting the profit and nonprofits not being able to distribute any of their surpluses.

Some strengths of worker cooperatives are their strong resiliency and high productivity (Perotin, 2016). This could be attributed to worker-members feeling committed and responsible to the company so that they put in place strategies that would allow them to ride out economic crises. This can include strategies such as reducing salaries. This flexibility on the workers end allowed many cooperatives to stay open even in the midst of hard economic times. Productivity has been reported higher in worker cooperatives (Perotin, 2016). Many times people may view everyone voting in decisions as taking up too much time in the workplace or even as an inefficient process, but there is actual evidence that higher productivity is the result.

Some weaknesses that worker cooperatives experience include the following: with everyone having an equal vote and a lack of traditional hierarchy, the concern arises of not having enough direction for the company's future. Workers voting rights can mitigate this, but with everyone having a say in the decisions, there is the possibility of arriving at no conclusions in decision-making.

Mission Drift and Accountability

The different models presented in this chapter offer varying levels of accountability and governance. For example, with the Benefit Corporation and the L3C, the directors can change the social component of the mission, diverting resources to the revenue-generating aspects of the company with little impact to the tax and legal status of the organization. However, the formation of a Community Contribution Corporation prevents the owners from diverting too far away from the social mission by placing a cap on the distributions that the members can take as a result of the company profits (Ebrahim, A., Battilana, J., & Mair, J., 2014).

Considerations

There are other things to consider when determining the best legal structure for a social enterprise. UnLtd (UnLTd, Social Entrepreneurship Awards Toolkit, 2010) provides a good list of issues that should be taken into account when determining the best legal structure for a social enterprise. These types of questions should be asked by the social entrepreneur before he or she decides which type of structure best fits their strategy.

Personal Liability

Personal liability is the degree to which an individual is held personally liable for the financial loss of the enterprise. Losses can be a result of decreased revenue or lawsuits related to the business activities. The level of personal liability available for the legal structure should factor into the decision regarding the appropriate legal and tax status for the enterprise.

Ownership

Ownership of the company is another consideration; as this will affect decision-making and the ability to control shares. For example, the ownership of a cooperative is different than the ownership of a for-profit or nonprofit company. The decision-making and ownership of the company factor into the model, as well as the focus and mission of the organization. An individual or entrepreneur who desires to maintain a high level of control and ownership should factor this in when considering the best structure and model for the social enterprise.

Funding: Both Short and Long Term

The funding aspect of an organization is vital to the mission and sustainability of a business model. Depending on how the funds will be gained will determine the level or the type of legal structure chosen. For example, if a social entrepreneur desires to rely heavily on charitable donations and grants for start-up funding and revenue, a nonprofit model would be an option. However, if the entrepreneur would like to develop a model whereby investors are allowed to share in the long-term revenue of the company, a for-profit model might be a better option. Short-term start-up financing should be separate from the long-term revenue-generating aspects of the organization. The start-up funding and the cost associated with purchasing materials and hiring workers is a separate model, an aspect of the business operations compared to the long-term revenue-generating aspects of the company. Both the short-term start-up cost and the long-term revenue-generating aspects of the company should be taken into consideration. This aspect of financing will be discussed later on in this book.

Governance

Similar to the ownership dynamic of an organization, the governance is a description of who is responsible for the overall strategy and the obligations of the company both to the legal requirements as well as the social goals. Whether an organization is governed by a board of directors or is a cooperative in which members make decisions, the governance will affect the long-term decision-making and strategic direction of the organization.

Profit Distribution

Social enterprises, by definition, should be generating profits. How these profits are used is a function of the model and the legal structure. As discussed previously, a nonprofit can generate profits, but the use of the profits is limited by the legal structure. These limitations factor into the model and the revenue options for the entrepreneur.

There is a real problem in the United States with teenagers not finishing high school despite administration and even organization's attempted interventions. The United States used to have the highest graduation rate, but in recent years has fallen to 18th among the top 24 industrialized nations.

This is not a problem that could be solved alone. That is why one nonprofit, in the Cincinnati area, has had tremendous success in recent years. Strive aims at bringing together leaders in the area to together tackle the education problem. These leaders include heads of foundations, city officials, school district representatives and executive directors of many education related organizations. Strive works with all these leaders to improve the lives of students from their infancy through career. With the variety of different sectors coming together and working with one infrastructure for one common purpose, Strive is a prime example of having a collective impact.

Research shows that for a collective impact to be successful there must be five inputs working together. First, there must be a common agenda. With many organizations working together it is easy for miscommunication to occur. But the collective group should agree on the common end goal of the initiative. It should be noted that not all members have to agree with each other's stances on certain aspects of the issue, but they all have to be in agreement of the end result that is trying to be achieved and then work together in a joint approach to solve this problem together.

Second, it is important that everyone is in agreement of the measurement systems. Everyone needs to be on the same page of what is aspects of the collective are being measured so that nobody loses sight of the end goal, and so that each member is held accountable.

Third, it is crucial that a collective impact has mutually reinforcing activities to stay successful. This means that all participants encourage each other to excel in their specific area, in a way that helps support others initiatives. Everyone needs to work together not only doing their own work to the best of their ability, but doing so in accordance with the overall goal.

Fourth, there needs to be continuous communication for success. It is essential that participants meet on a regular basis to not only discuss matters but to build a mutual trust with one another. If trust is not present, then succeeding in the overall mission will be more unlikely. It is important that all participants attend meetings on a regular basis, and it is just as important that there is an open line of communication between meetings through web chats or emails.

Finally, it is important that there is a backbone organization for support. This means that a separate organization exists to manage the initiatives of the collective impact. This translates into a single organization planning, managing, facilitating, and supporting any administrative details of the mission. To ensure that each participating member is doing all they can do for the collective mission, it is critical that a backbone organization exists.

It should be noted that many organizations try to have an isolated impact, but many times that does not have as much as an impact as a collective impact will have. The reason being, social problems are bigger than any one organization, and without the collective action of many organizations trying to mitigate this problem together it is unlikely that the problem will be solved (Kania & Kramer, 2011).

Kania, J., & Kramer, M. (2011). Collective Impact (SSIR). Retrieved February 02, 2018, from https://ssir.org/articles/entry/collective_impact

References

Brakman Reiser, D. (2013). Theorizing forms for social enterprise. *Emory Law Journal, 62*, 681–739.

British Columbia—Ministry of Finance, 2017. QUESTIONS AND ANSWERS COMMUNITY CONTRIBUTION COMPANIES (C3s). http://www.fin.gov. bc.ca/prs/ccc/caq.htm

Brown, J. (2006). Equity finance for social enterprises. *Social Enterprise Journal, 2*(1), 73–81. https://doi.org/10.1108/17508610680000714

Community Foundations. (n.d.). Retrieved February 10, 2018, from https://www. cof.org/foundation-type/community-foundations-taxonomy

Community interest companies: case studies. (n.d.). Retrieved February 10, 2018, from https://www.gov.uk/government/collections/ community-interest-companies-case-studies

Daly, S. (2008). Institutional innovation in philanthropy: Community foundations in the UK. *Voluntas, 19*(3), 219–241. https://doi.org/10.1007/s11266-008-9067-7

Ebrahim, A., Battilana, J., & Mair, J. (2014). The governance of social enterprises: Mission drift and accountability challenges in hybrid organizations. *Research in Organizational Behavior, 34*(January 2016), 81–100. https://doi.org/10.1016/j. riob.2014.09.001

Fitzgerald, M. (2015, February 10). For Warby Parker, Free Glasses Equals Clear Company Vision. Retrieved February 10, 2018, from https://www.entrepreneur. com/article/242437

Goodwill, *About Us*. http://www.goodwill.org/about-us/

Haugh, H. (2005). A research agenda for social entrepreneurship. *Social Enterprise Journal, 1*(1), 1–12.

ICF GHK. (2013). Growing the social investment market: the landscape and economic impact, (July), 1–72.

Johnson, G., & Jones, D. (1994). *Community Foundations* (1994 EO CPE Text). Retrieved from https://www.irs.gov/pub/irs-tege/eotopick94.pdf

Kania, J., & Kramer, M. (2011). Collective Impact (SSIR). Retrieved February 02, 2018, from https://ssir.org/articles/entry/collective_impact

Macalister, T. (2008, July 15). The rise and fall of flagship refuse firm ECT. Retrieved February 10, 2018, from https://www.theguardian.com/society/2008/jul/16/socialenterprises.recycling

Nicholls, A. (2010). Institutionalizing social entrepreneurship in regulatory space: Reporting and disclosure by community interest companies. *Accounting, Organizations and Society, 35*(4), 394–415. https://doi.org/10.1016/j.aos.2009.08.001

Office of the Regulator of Community Interest Companies: Information and guidance notes: Chapter 1: Introduction. (2016). Retrieved from https://www.gov.uk/government/uploads/system/uploads/attachment_data/file/626088/cic-12-1333-community-interest-companies-guidance-chapter-1-introduction.pdf

Office of the Regulator of Community Interest Companies: Information and guidance notes: Chapter 6: The Asset Lock. (2016). Retrieved from https://www.gov.uk/government/uploads/system/uploads/attachment_data/file/605418/14-1089-community-interest-companies-chapter-6-the-asset-lock.pdf

Perotin, V. (2016). *What Do We Really Know About Worker Co-Operatives? Co-Operatives UK.* https://doi.org/10.1016/j.csm.2008.10.002

Reiser, D. B. (2011). Benefit corporations—a sustainable form of organization? *Wake Forest Law Review, 46*(3), 591–625. https://doi.org/10.1525/sp.2007.54.1.23.

Reiser, D. B. (2012). Theorizing Forms For Social Enterprise. *Emory LJ, 62*: 681. Retrieved from http://law.emory.edu/elj/_documents/volumes/62/4/contents/reiser.pdf

Rothschild, J. (2009). Workers' cooperatives and social enterprise: A forgotten route to social equity and democracy. *American Behavioral Scientist, 52*(7), 1023–1041. https://doi.org/10.1177/0002764208327673

Thomley, B., Wood, D., Grace, K., & Sarah, S. (2011). Impact investing: A framework for policy design and analysis. *Pacific Community*, 104. Retrieved from http://www.rockefellerfoundation.org/uploads/files/88fdd93f-b778-461e-828c-5c526ffed184-impact.pdf

UnLtd. (2010). *Social Entrepreneurship Awards Toolkit.* Retrieved from https://unltd.org.uk/wp-content/uploads/2012/12/full-toolkit1.pdf

Virginia Benefit Corporation How-To-Guide: Incorporating as a Benefit Corporation Step-by-Step. (2013). Retrieved from http://benefitcorp.net/sites/default/files/documents/Virginia_Benefit_Corp_How-To_Guide_.pdf

Wilburn, K., & Wilburn, R. (2014). The double bottom line: Profit and social benefit. *Business Horizons, 57*(1), 11–20. https://doi.org/10.1016/j.bushor.2013.10.001

Witkin, Jim (15 January 2009). "The L3C: A More Creative Capitalism". *The Triple Pundit*. Retrieved 16 Jan 2018. https://www.triplepundit.com/2009/01/the-l3c-a-more-creative-capitalism/

Government Publishing Office-IRS https://www.gpo.gov/fdsys/pkg/CFR-2012-title26-vol3/pdf/CFR-2012-title26-vol3-sec1-170A-9.pdf

PART 3:
Management of
Social Enterprises

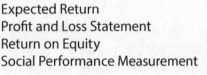

Learning Outcomes

- Summarize some of the most commonly used measurements for social impact
- Distinguish between activities and outcomes in social enterprises
- Discover resources related to social impact measurement
- Understand traditional financial measurements of organization effectiveness

Key Terms

Alignment	Expected Return
BACO Ratio	Profit and Loss Statement
Balance Sheet	Return on Equity
Balanced Scorecard	Social Performance Measurement

Introduction

Any organization or business must have a way to determine whether or not the resources used to accomplish the organizational mission and goals are being most effectively used. There are a number of different ways that traditional entrepreneurial organizations seek to determine effectiveness and efficiencies. These methods include formulas such as return on equity, stock price, or how quickly they turn over their inventory. Companies also analyze statements such as their income statement, balance sheet, and statement of cash flows (Arena, Azzone, Bengo, 2015). However, when we look at these traditional methods, we must ask if they operate the same way in a social enterprise for social entrepreneurs as they do for traditional entrepreneurs. How exactly do we measure social impact? Can all social impacts be measured in the same way as financial revenue?

> **Return on Equity**
>
> A measure of how much profit is made per dollar of investment from shareholders.

> **Balance Sheet**
>
> A financial statement that provides a picture of the firm's assets and liabilities at a certain moment in time, used to monitor and analyze the firm's financial position.

How individual organizations answer these questions will determine the degree to which they can effectively measure return on investment for resources, including human and financial, as well as being able to communicate and understand whether or not their efforts are actually bringing about the changes they are seeking. In this chapter we will look at some of the traditional methods and models used by entrepreneurs and businesses to measure effectiveness and look at ways in which social entrepreneurs are developing unique methods to accomplish the same things for their ends.

As new nonprofits and social enterprises continue to move into the forefront, the need for accountability and public trust in these organizations must be considered if the social entrepreneur is going to be able to continue to engage consumers as well as investors (Ebrahim & Rangan, 2010).

As we looked at in previous chapters, the mission of the company should be aligned with the established understanding of the central social problem to be solved, as well as the financing method that will be used for the long-term sustained health of the organization.

Any business executive needs to know how to direct resources in a manner consistent with the company's mission, while taking into account feedback and data on whether or not the company's mission is being effectively met with the current resource allocation. Many times social enterprises and social entrepreneurs move into a situation without a clear understanding of how effectiveness will be measured.

As a means of introduction to business performance, let's look at a few of the typical measurements utilized by conventional entrepreneurs.

Profit and Loss Statement (Income Statement)

Profit and Loss (P&L) Statement

A financial statement that shows how profitable the firm is over the course of a year.

The **profit and loss (P&L) statement** is one of the financial documents that every public company is required to release at the end of each fiscal year. The purpose of the P&L statement is to show how profitable the firm is over the course of the year. The firm's earnings before interest and taxes (EBIT) is calculated by adding the firm's total revenue and all other sources of income and subtracting the costs and charges for depreciation. The rest of the statement is used to describe how the firm used these earnings. Deductions will be made for interest expenses and income tax, and the remaining amount is labeled as the net income. The main goal of the P&L statement is to quantify the firm's ability to increase revenue, or decrease costs, and as a result, increase profits.

Balance Sheet

The balance sheet provides a picture of the firm's assets and liabilities at a certain moment in time and is used to monitor and analyze the firm's financial position. All the company's assets are listed on the left-hand side from most liquid to least liquid, with liquid meaning available cash, or the ability for an asset to be converted to cash quickly. The right-hand side contains the firm's liabilities, or the sources of financing the firm used to purchase their assets. Liabilities are listed in two categories, current liabilities and long-term liabilities. Current liabilities are those that are most likely to be paid off quickly and include borrowings and accounts payable while long-term liabilities include any debt that is due after a year. The remaining amount belongs to the shareholders as equity. Many of the common financial ratios used to measure company performance, liquidity, and efficiency are calculated using this document.

Return on Assets

$$ROA = \frac{\text{After Tax Operating Income}}{\text{Total Assets}}$$

Return on assets (ROA) is a measure of how profitable a company is based on the resources it owns. After-tax operating income is calculated by adding together the net income and after-tax interest. ROA is generally used more by management because it is a measure of how well the firm is using its resources, not how much investors receive based on their input. One of the most useful applications for ROA is to analyze the effectiveness of different capital structures between firms (Brealey, 2017).

Return on Equity

$$ROE = \frac{\text{Net Income}}{\text{Sales}} \times \frac{\text{Sales}}{\text{Assets}} \times \frac{\text{Assets}}{\text{Shareholder's Equity}} = \frac{\text{Net Income}}{\text{Shareholder's Equity}}$$

Return on equity is a measure of how much profit is made per dollar of investment from shareholders. Net income is measured over the full fiscal year, and shareholder's equity does not include preferred stock. ROE is useful when comparing firms in the same industry because it shows how efficient the firm is in using the money it receives from investors. It is most useful when viewed over time to observe which direction the company is heading, but there are a couple of issues to be conscious about. ROE can often be manipulated by organizations and cause them to appear like they are performing better than they actually are (Mohr, 2017). For example, ROE takes into account the firm's equity investments, but not the firm's debt. Therefore, if the company takes on large sums of debt, the income generated from that debt would increase net income, and as a result increase ROE. If investors only considered ROE, it would appear that the firm was doing well even though the firm was being destroyed by the massive amounts of debt they incurred. Therefore, ROE is most useful when used with other financial ratios.

Profit Margin

$$\text{Profit Margin} = \frac{\text{Net Income}}{\text{Sales}}$$

$$\text{Operating Profit Margin} = \frac{\text{After Tax Operating Income}}{\text{Sales}}$$

Profit margin is a firm's net income divided by its sales (Brealey, 2017). However, this value is not always an accurate representation of the firm's profitability because interest paid on debt financing is subtracted from net income. This causes firms that use debt financing to seem less profitable than those who do not. Using the after-tax operating income instead of income negates this issue by adding back in the after-tax debt interest. This value is called the operating profit margin.

Earnings Per Share

$$EPS = \frac{\text{Net Income} - \text{Preferred Dividends}}{\text{Average Shares Outstanding}}$$

Earnings per share (EPS) is the portion of income generated by the firm that is distributed for each outstanding share of common stock and is another way to measure the profitability of a firm. Since the number of outstanding shares of common stock often changes over time, it is best to use the average shares outstanding when calculating this value (Jewell, 2016). EPS is very important because it is the variable that has the greatest effect on the value of a firm's shares. This is important to investors because an increase in profit for a firm could be misleading if the firm also increases its number of shares outstanding.

Balanced Scorecard

Balanced Scorecard

A document that lays out the big picture goals of the organization and the initiatives the organization will use to achieve those goals.

See Balanced Scorecard here: http://www.balancedscorecard.org/BSC-Basics/About-the-Balanced-Scorecard

The balanced scorecard is a document that lays out the big picture goals of the organization and the initiatives the organization will use to achieve those goals. This document is useful for communicating what the organization wishes to accomplish, focus everyone involved on the organization's goals, lay out which aspects of the organization should be prioritized, and measure progress toward achieving organizational objectives. The balanced scorecard lays out four perspectives from which we view the organization: financial, the customer or stakeholder (satisfaction), internal process (efficiency), and organizational capacity (knowledge and innovation) (What is the Balanced Scorecard?, n.d). Strategy mapping is a key element of the balanced scorecard as it helps to clearly communicate the value adding aspects of the organization. The strategy map shows how each of the four organizational perspectives affect the others. For example, improvements in organizational capacity lead to more efficient and higher quality internal processes, which leads to improved products and services being delivered to the customer and realization of the organization's financial objectives. Another important aspect of the balanced scorecard is development of key performance indicators (KPIs). Every organizational objective must have a clearly defined and measurable KPI so that progress toward these objectives can be quantified and tracked.

Social Performance Measurement

Social Performance Measurement

The method by which a social enterprise measures the effect of their activities on the desired social change.

The previous measurements and financial statements help to show us how a traditional enterprise will operate and measure financial health and stability. However, when it comes to social problems, it is helpful to be able to understand how these financial measurements are being used in addressing the social need. Keep in mind that the social performance of the organization should flow directly from the established mission and business model that best fits the solution. For the social performance, we will look at some of the existing standards that can be used to measure the impact of the social enterprise.

Logic Model

As discussed in the previous chapter on opportunity recognition, it is important for there to be a logical flow between the problem, the cause of the problem, the solution to the problem, and the mission of the social enterprise. This creates a type of logic model that can help to provide a framework for how the effectiveness of the social enterprise will work and whether or not the enterprise is actually accomplishing the mission. The Center for Social Impact Strategy at the University of Pennsylvania (Logic Model Toolkit) provides a logical model that is intended to align the activities of the social enterprise and the resulting impacts. Many of the social reporting models will use some sort of description for inputs, activities, outputs, outcomes, and impacts, to describe the social changes that are taking place as a result of the activities of the social enterprise. We will describe each below.

Inputs

In social reporting, inputs represent the resources that are used in creating the program or treatment that has been identified to address the social need. For example, if there is a social enterprise that is focused on providing low-cost education services to underserved communities, the input will be the teachers, facilities, curriculum, etc. that goes into providing the classes. The inputs should be effectively measured and the costs associated with the inputs factored into any assessment of the organization.

Activities

The activities in the logic model include those specific actions that an organization takes to help bring about the desired impact. The activities include the sales, trainings, or presentations that are created or brought about by the organization. These can also be workshops or delivered goods or services.

Outputs

The outputs for the activities are a measurement for the activities. For example, if the activity is a training, how many attended the training? It can also measure the number of units produced or the amount of money granted to stakeholders.

Outcomes

The outcomes are a way to determine or measure what changes occur as a result of the activity. For example, if an organization offers a training on how to prepare for an interview, the outcome might be to determine if the attendees were able to take what they learned and use it to obtain a job. Does the activity produce a positive outcome for the beneficiaries?

Impact

When looking at impact, what we want to determine is how those outcomes benefit the larger social context. Using the above example, if the individuals are using the training to obtain jobs, what is the larger social impact to their employment? This impact should be consistent with the overall mission and established goals of the organization. It is this alignment that is key to helping the company ensure that their performance measurements are consistent with their identified model of business and social change.

Bayaud Enterprises

Bayaud Enterprises helps individuals with disabilities move back into the work force after being discharged from the hospital. Bayaud Enterprises has adopted an individualized method for measuring impact through outcomes. When they first bring someone into their program, they sit down with the individual to discuss their barriers to gaining employment. They then develop a plan that ranks these barriers in terms of importance from the individual's perspective, and each barrier is designated a "red light" status. As progress is made within each area, they adjust the status to a "yellow light" and finally to a "green light" when the issue is resolved. This process helps guide the individual toward paid employment, medical benefits, reliable transportation, food stamp acquisition, social security benefits, and more. Bayaud Enterprises uses these services to help the people in their programs to obtain and keep employment to achieve their ultimate indicator of success, a secure living situation and support system for their participants. "My belief, based on working in the 'work therapy' program at Ft. Logan (*Ft. Logan Mental Health Center in Denver*) was that individuals valued the opportunity to work, and for many it was the most important part of their 'treatment' day in the hospital." "Seeing that partnering with the private sector opened up new employment options inspired us to integrate both a work center environment (using sub-contracted work from the business community) and a transitional employment model to provide daily, paid employment, plus benefits, for people with limited options due to either the barriers of their illness or lacking the connections to gain a community job"- David E. Henninger (Executive Director).

Can All Impacts Be Measured?

When we look at the impact and the long-term cultural change that social entrepreneurs and enterprises seek, it can be a challenge to directly attribute the activities of the organization to the impact. It is similar to the distinction between correlation and causation. For example, if a rights-based or advocacy group seeks to make changes and impact the cultural dialogue regarding race or gender or disability, it can be tough to draw a straight line between the activities and outputs of the organization and the broad-based social impact. While the organization may contribute to the change in social in some way, such as in attitudes toward a particular group or situation, effectively measuring that contribution can be challenging, if not impossible. Conversely, a social enterprise that is engaged in providing food to an underserved population can more directly measure the impact their activities had on the problem of hunger within that target group.

It may be helpful to then think of outcomes and impact on a continuum, or as a part of a scale, where the impacts can be more directly and immediately measured, are on one end of the spectrum and more nebulous or less causal.

Easily Quantifiable   **Difficult to Quantify**

Social Entrepreneur Measurements

SRS: Social Reporting Standard

The Social Reporting Standard (SRS) was published by the Social Reporting Initiative in a push to make social and nonprofit organizations more transparent to the public, and as a result, further legitimize the work that they do. The SRS lays out the framework for social organizations to clearly and effectively engage in results-based reporting. This framework is broken down into three parts. Part A presents an overview of the report along with the vision of the organization and the offers they will be reporting on. Part B is where the problem the organization is addressing is defined in detail, and where any previously attempted solutions to the problem are addressed. Part B also includes a report on all resources used during the reporting period, the work performed, the results from the organization's efforts, and any measures used to evaluate those results. Finally, any future plans and chances and risks are documented before giving an overview of the organizational structure. Part C provides an outline of the organizational framework, governance, and financial and accounting principles. Following the SRS structure will allow the organization to document the social issue and its origins, the organizational vision, the IOOI impact chain (Input, Output, Outcome, and Impact), and the organization's financial and organizational framework (Social Reporting Standard, 2014).

SROI: Social Return on Investment

Social return on investment (SROI) is a concept developed by the Robert Development Fund that helps organizations measure and report the environmental, financial, and social value of their work. SROI, as a value, is defined as the net present value of the benefits divided by the net present value of the investment, but this is not the only way in which SROI should be viewed. It uses both quantitative and qualitative approaches to describe overall social benefits in financial terms. In 2007 the New Economics Foundation (NEF) released its own approach to SROI in which they have four main areas of focus: making stakeholders central to the process, developing an interactive map that describes how the organization is working toward its mission (inputs, outputs, outcomes, and impacts), gathering relevant and useful information, and developing a method for analyzing how much change can be attributed to the organization rather than that which would have happened naturally, or deadweight (New Economic Foundation, 2007).

The NEF found that SROI is helpful to organizations in a few different ways. First, it increases accountability by making the social value adding methods used by the organization transparent to all stakeholders. Second, it helps organizations improve their decision-making process by analyzing current projects for strength and weaknesses and identifying where improvements need to be made. Finally, it makes analyzing the societal change the organization creates relatively quick and cost effective (New Economic Foundation, 2007). However, it is not a perfect system. One of the main concerns with SROI is that not every impact an organization has can be measured and displayed as a numerical value, and organizations that have little experience with impact measurement and reporting can often have a difficult time implementing it (Mcloughlin, 2009).

BACO Ratio

> **BACO (Best Available Charitable Option) Ratio**
>
> A way to compare the impact of direct investment of funds and donations to charitable organizations to solve social issues.

The best available charitable option (BACO) ratio was developed by Acumen Fund, a 501(c)3 social venture that uses a blend of market-oriented approaches and philanthropy to provide necessities to people around the world affected by poverty. Acumen Fund invests patient capital in entrepreneurs, whose ideas are directed toward reducing poverty, and trains them to get the most out of their businesses (https://acumen.org/about/).

The BACO ratio was developed as a way to compare the impact of direct investment of funds and donations to charitable organizations to solve social issues. This ratio is most effectively used in comparing alternatives that seek to solve the same issue, rather than as a broad comparison for social return across a multitude of causes. It is calculated by comparing the net cost per number of units of social impact for each option (The Best Available Charitable Option, 2007). For example, say you were comparing the effects of giving a loan to a company whose work helps fight hunger in your hometown, and a similar donation to a charitable organization that works to solve the same issue. If estimates predict that it would cost $10,000 to feed 10,000 people through the loan, it would cost the investor $1.00 per unit of social impact.

Similarly, if estimates predict that it would cost $20,000 to feed 10,000 people through the charitable donation, then it would cost the investor $2.00 per unit of social impact. Comparing these values results in a BACO ratio of 2. In other words, it is twice as cost effective to give the loan than to donate to the charitable organization.

However, there are a few issues that come with using this method. First, it does not evaluate the long-term effects of the different options but focuses on what the immediate effect of the investment will be. Second, the accuracy of this method depends largely on selecting the right charitable organization to compare the investment to, which can often be difficult. Finally, the BACO ratio can compare investments, but it cannot be used to evaluate how those investments affect the overall issue the organization wishes to solve (The Best Available Charitable Option, 2007). Using the example given above, the BACO ratio can help decide which option is most efficient at feeding people. However, it cannot compare how this will impact overall poverty levels compared to investing in another solution to solve poverty such as low-income housing opportunities.

The Center for High Impact Philanthropy (CHIP) has the goal of connecting philanthropists with organizations that seek to make an impact in society. They achieve this by being a reputable resource for philanthropists to use to determine which organization they should give to. Each year CHIP comes out with a High Impact Giving Guide, in which they identify nonprofits that achieve a positive impact at a practical price. This guide has nonprofits organized into three sections: health, poverty, and education. CHIP will evaluate nonprofits by working with experts at the university. They will call on any experts they feel are necessary to properly evaluate an organization. They vet all the nonprofits in the guide by the impact the organization is making and how cost effective that organization is (The Center For High Impact Philanthropy, n.d.).

ER: Expected Return

Expected Return was developed in 2008 by the William and Flora Hewlett Foundation as a way to help philanthropists make better investment decisions through the analysis of quantitative data. Using the Expected Return method helps identify which opportunities will yield the highest returns, focus a diverse portfolio of strategies on a single overarching goal, reduce bias

Expected Return

An estimate found by multiplying the outcome, likelihood of success, and the philanthropic contribution, then dividing by the cost.

in the grant-making process, and find the most efficient usage of funds to impact populations locally and abroad. Most importantly, it provides a way for philanthropists to consistently document and evaluate the impact of their investment decisions. Before calculating Expected Return, it is important to clearly define the parameters of the decision being investigated. This includes choosing the metric with which each decision will be measured, fully defining the geographic location where impact is going to be measured, and tightening the range of strategies that will be considered in the analysis (Making Every Dollar Count, 2008).

The value of Expected Return is found by multiplying the outcome, likelihood of success, and the philanthropic contribution, and then dividing by the cost. The outcome is found by estimating what the direct and indirect benefits to society will be if the strategy goes as planned. Likelihood of success quantifies the risk associated with the investment. This includes the probability that the strategy implemented is linked to the desired outcome, the probability that the organization receiving the grant will have the capacity and skill needed to succeed, and the probability that a various number of external factors will restrict the outcome. The philanthropic contribution is defined as the percentage of all financial and non-financial resources, such as leadership, that are required from a specific organization. Lastly, the cost is a combination of the financial resources needed to implement the strategy and any overhead costs needed for the organization to operate, such as employee salaries. The cost is calculated only for the investment made by the philanthropy being observed (Making Every Dollar Count, 2008).

The Robin Hood Foundation has had a goal of creating a methodology that would allow them to measure the success of their investments by comparing grants that are dissimilar in nature. They seek to compare, what many would call, apples to oranges. For example, they offer grants that cover programs such as job-training, school, and health. Their overall mission as a foundation is to reduce poverty in New York City, so they want to look at how each grant ranks overall to their mission. To do this, they will look at existing research and knowledge of peers, and make educated assumptions. Essentially, they come up with a benefit-cost ratio for programs. The benefit portion of the ratio will obviously change per program but the concept will stay the same. For example, for a grant that is given for job-training, the benefit may be calculated estimating how much the earnings of all job training recipients will increase over their lifetimes now that they have had the training. The cost portion of the ratio is simply the dollar amount of the grant. It should be noted that these ratios alone do not make up the whether or not a grant will be given to a particular cause, but they do play a vital role (Weinstein, 2007).

Social Enterprise Balanced Scorecard

As discussed previously, the balanced scorecard is a document geared toward helping organizations clearly define their mission, map out the strategies they will implement to achieve their mission, and measure their results. However, leadership in nonprofit organizations and public-sector agencies were having trouble adopting this system because financial success was not their primary objective. The first steps in remedying this came from Kaplan and Norton (2001) who recommend additions to the model for organizations who have run into this issue.

One of the main points Kaplan and Norton make is that, in the nonprofit organization, defining who the customer is can be tricky. In the private sector the distinction is simple; the customer receives the product or service by purchasing it themselves. However, in a nonprofit the recipient does not purchase the product or service, but rather it is supplied to them through contributions from donors. This highlights the need for nonprofits to develop specific objectives and strategies directed toward benefiting both the recipient and the donor, and ultimately fostering the organization's mission.

Somers (2005) furthers the adaptation started by Kaplan and Norton by introducing the Social Enterprise Balanced Scorecard (SEBC). The major changes in Somers' model include the addition of social objectives above the financial perspective, a broadening of the financial perspective to concentrate on sustainability, and an expansion of the customer perspective to include a larger group of stakeholders.

This version of the balanced scorecard is a representation of an organization's key components from a financial perspective and a social perspective. After identifying the key components of the organization, it is important to identify, from both the financial and social perspective, what drives the organization to achieve those components. This allows a company to look at which stakeholders and processes play a crucial role in executing their mission.

The Social Enterprise Balanced Scorecard approach, looks for a company to create a strategy map, as pictured below. After creating a strategy map, the organization needs to create a performance measurement schedule. This will allow the organization to look at each component of the map and its objectives and determine how success is measured. An organization can determine how setting targets for performance and time measure success. With each section of the map being measured, a company can ensure that it is maintaining its overall objectives and identify areas that need improvement.

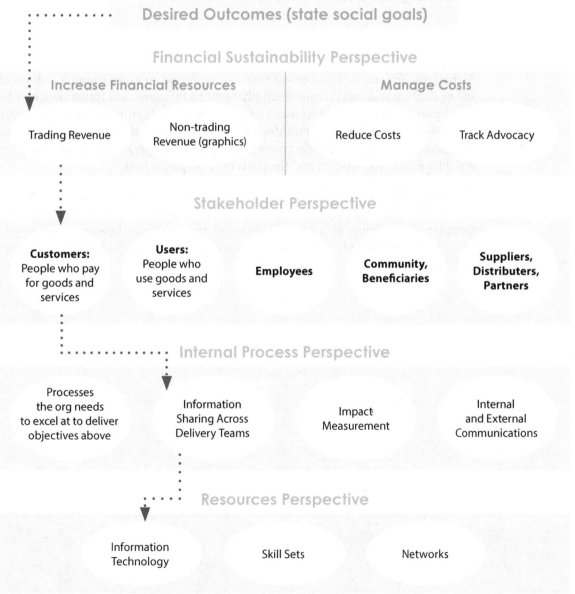

Figure 6.2 Social enterprise balanced scorecard model

The Impact Reporting and Investment Standards (IRIS) was set in place by the Global Impact Investing Network (GIIN). GIIN is a nonprofit that seeks to increase impact investing's effectiveness, and they offer IRIS to help support transparency, credibility, and accountability for those seeking to make impact investments. IRIS offers a generally accepted performance metrics to measure the performance of an investor's investment. These metrics allow one to measure an investment's financial, operational, product, sector, social and environmental performance. Not only can a user see how their impact ranks in relation to a certain sector, IRIS allows an individual to view metrics irrespective of their impact segment or sector (IRIS Metrics, n.d.).

Implementing a Culture of Measurement

A challenge for many social enterprises can be found in establishing a culture of self-evaluation and measurement. Simply having a measurement framework may be insufficient in improving outcomes and performance (Ebrahim and Rangan, 2010). It is therefore incumbent upon the decision makers to begin to establish performance measurements early, and to help create a culture whereby performance measurement is tightly knit to the mission and the goals of the organization.

This idea of alignment is a key component to any entrepreneurial endeavor whether it is social or conventional. Making sure that the mission and methods and measurement are all in alignment is a key factor to helping determine how resources should be utilized and diverted. Especially in the early stages of a company, where resources may be limited.

References

Arena, M., Azzone, G., & Bengo, I. (2015). Performance Measurement for Social Enterprises. *Voluntas, 26*(2), 649–672. https://doi.org/10.1007/s11266-013-9436-8

Brealey, R. A., Myers, S. C., & Marcus, A. J. (2017). Fundamentals of Corporate Finance (9th ed.). New York, NY: McGraw-Hill.

CHIP. Center for High Impact Philanthropy. Cost per impact. Retreived from https://www.impact.upenn.edu

Ebrahim, A., & Rangan, V. K. (2010). The limits of nonprofit impact: A contingency framework for measuring social performance. *Social Enterprise Initiative, Harvard Business School, 8*(1), 1–6. https://doi.org/10.5465/AMBPP.2010.54500944

IRIS Metrics. (n.d.). Retrieved June 4, 2018, from https://iris.thegiin.org/metrics

Jewell, J. J., & Mankin, J. A. (2016). What is your EPS? Issues in computing and interpreting earnings per share. *Academy of Accounting and Financial Studies Journal, 20*(3). Retrieved February 15, 2018.

Kaplan, R. S., & Norton, D. P. (2001). Transforming the Balanced Scorecard from Performance Measurement to Strategic Management: Part I. Accounting Horizons, *15*(1), 87–104. doi:10.2308/acch.2001.15.1.87

Logic Model Toolkit. (2018) Retrieved from http://studio.socialimpactstrategy.org/

Making Every Dollar Count: How expected return can transform philanthropy (2008). Retrieved from http://www.hewlett.org/wp-content/uploads/2016/08/Making_Every_Dollar_Count.pdf

Mcloughlin, J., Kaminski, J., Sodagar, B., Khan, S., Harris, R., Arnaudo, G., & Brearty, S. M. (2009). A strategic approach to social impact measurement of social enterprises. *Social Enterprise Journal, 5*(2), 154–178. doi:10.1108/17508610910981734

Mohr, A. (2017, September 26). The Disadvantages of Using Return on Equity. Retrieved February 15, 2018, from https://bizfluent.com/info-8609431-disadvantages-using-return-equity.html

New Economics Foundation (Nef) (2007). Measuring Real Value: a DIY guide to Social Return on Investment. Retrieved from: http://www.neweconomics.org/sites/neweconomics.org/files/Measuring_Real_Value.pdf

Scheuerle, T., & Schmitz, B. (2015). Inhibiting factors of scaling up the impact of social entrepreneurial organizations – A comprehensive framework and empirical results for Germany. *Journal of Social Entrepreneurship, 676*(March 2016), 1–35. https://doi.org/10.1080/19420676.2015.1086409

Social Reporting Standard (SRS). (2014). *SRS: Social Reporting Standard—Guide to results- based reporting.* Retrieved from: http://www.social-reporting-standard. de/wp-content/uploads/2014/08/SRS-guidelines_en.pdf

Somers, A. B. (2005). Shaping the balanced scorecard for use in UK social enterprises. *Social Enterprise Journal, 1*(1), 43–56. doi:10.1108/17508610580000706

The Best Available Charitable Option. (2007, January). Retrieved February 19, 2018, from https://acumen.org/wp-content/uploads/2013/03/BACO-Concept-Paper-final.pdf

The Center For High Impact Philanthropy. (n.d.). Retrieved June 4, 2018, from https://www.impact.upenn.edu/

Weinstein, M. M. (2007). Measuring Success: How the Robin Hood Foundation Estimates the Impact of Grants. http://readynation.s3.amazonaws.com/docs/ivk/iikmeeting_slides200711weinstein.pdf

What is the Balanced Scorecard? (n.d.). Retrieved February 15, 2018, from http://www.balancedscorecard.org/BSC-Basics/About-the-Balanced-Scorecard

Chapter 7

Organizational Behavior in Social Enterprise

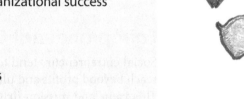

Learning Outcomes

- Describe the role of personnel in the social enterprise
- Summarize the impact of team dynamics on an organization
- Identify strengths and weaknesses of virtual teams
- Connect the aspects of organizational culture to organizational success

Key Terms

Intrapreneurship

Mission Drift

Organization Behavior

Organizational Culture

Personnel

Virtual Teams

Volunteers

Rethreaded

Rethreaded is a faith-based, 501(c)(3) nonprofit organization based in Jacksonville, Florida, that produces and sells scarves, jewelry, bags, and more. Rethreaded operates with the mission of providing support for women around the world who have been affected by addiction, violence, human trafficking, and prostitution. They provide women in the Jacksonville area a three-month job training program where they can feel safe and get the help they need to recover from their traumatic experiences. They currently employ twelve survivors and five non-survivors full time and have plans to add another eight full-time staff members this year. Rethreaded also partners with organizations around the world that seek to end the cycle of sex trafficking through employment in the fashion apparel manufacturing industry by acting as a distributor for their products. Today they have helped to preserve the freedom of over 2,200 women internationally.

Rethreaded founder Kristin Keen spent five years in Kolkata, India, where she co-founded Sari Bari, a business that employs women impacted by the area's sex trade, to craft blankets and other products from traditional fabrics. When she returned to Jacksonville, she still felt called to fight the sex trade locally. This led to the creation of Rethreaded in 2012. Kristin believes that what these women need most is a safe environment where they can develop skills, earn a living, and be connected to a supportive community. Kristin also believes that businesses have an important role to play in the elimination of social issues.

Introduction

Introduction to Organizational Behavior

As social entrepreneurs begin, they may start with themselves as the only employee of the company. This allows them to be nimble, to make decisions quickly, and to implement those decisions in an efficient and effective manner. However, as the organization grows it will be important for the entrepreneur to be able to transition into a team-based and multipersonnel dynamic. In an organization with multiple individuals involved, an entrepreneur must deal with the dynamics associated with organizational behavior. In this chapter we will look at some of the aspects of organizational behavior and how they may uniquely affect a social enterprise.

> **Organizational Behavior**
>
> The interactions that takes place between members in an organization.

Entrepreneurial Organizational Behavior

Social entrepreneurs tend to be driven by a strong desire to engage in activities that reach beyond profits and ultimately impact individuals and society in a positive way. This value and mission drives and motivates the entrepreneur and helps define the organization as a whole and how it operates. This can take the form of individual and microlevel activities as well as team-based organizational and macrolevel activities (Greenberg, 2013). The social entrepreneur must be aware of these different dynamics and how each one of them, both macro- and microlevel challenges, can impact the success of the enterprise. By bringing into the discussion areas related to psychology, sociology, and leadership, a successful social entrepreneur can make the most of the individuals and teammates that they are surrounded with, moving toward a common vision.

> **Personnel**
>
> The individuals who are a formal part of an organization and contribute to the goals of the business.

Personnel

One of the ways that organizational behavior is most commonly discussed is in the area of personnel. The individuals that make up a social enterprise are one of the primary indicators of organizational health. How they are motivated, how they are lead, and how they interact and communicate is vital to the success of the organizational mission. In this section we will look at some of the different ways that personnel issues are reflected in organizations, and look at how they can be effectively used to drive forward the mission of the organization.

Hiring

As with any enterprise it is important to bring individuals on board who have a desire to contribute to the mission and vision of the organization, and not merely to collect a paycheck and exchange time for money. Social entrepreneurs should be sure to have the appropriate hiring policies in place to screen for applicants to make sure that they are motivated by the social value of the organization in addition to the financial health of the company. This may take the form of interviews or questionnaires related to not only the knowledge and competence of the individual, but also to the fit that the individual may have with company. It is also wise to keep in mind the social aspect of the company and how new employees may contribute to effectively engaging in the mission in a very specific way. An organization may hire individuals that can uniquely speak to the challenges of the target impact group. For example, if an organization is working primarily with individuals who have learning disabilities, hiring those people who have specific backgrounds related to teaching individuals with learning disabilities can have a unique impact on the social mission (Tan, Williams, Tan, 2005).

However, hiring in social enterprises can be a challenge, and finding and retaining the appropriate staff can be fraught with difficulties. This can be especially true in the early stages of a social enterprise, when there are limited human resources and few people assigned to multiple tasks. When individuals are asked to engage in activities and perform tasks that are outside of their skill set, it can lead to frustration for the individual as well as subpar performance in that particular aspect of the organization. Finding individuals who can perform a multitude of tasks and have a variety of effective skill sets is a challenge, and caution is in order to ensure that individuals are not set up for failure, or burned out due to work outside of their skill set (Gordon, 2016). A better idea, might be to look outside of the industry for individual skill sets and to outsource some skill sets whenever possible (Chang, 2011) especially for those types of projects that might have short-term needs such as logo design or event planning. It might be more expensive in the short-term, but the ultimate value of quality work will likely be worth the investment. Additionally, a social entrepreneur may have to deal with the challenge of hiring individuals who have the potential to do well, but haven't realized that potential yet, what Chang (2011) calls an "aspirational hire."

> This aspirational thinking is a crucial ingredient for any leader of social change. It also is the recipe for making bad hires. In my experience, the post-mortem on some bad hire often involves the phrase, "She can grow into this role" from the hiring process. While some level of aspirational thinking is good in hiring, the tolerances have to be much, much lower: A 50 percent success rate with your mission population is probably fantastic; a 50 percent success rate in hiring is definitely fatal. (Chang, 2011).

Volunteers

Management of volunteers is important for many social enterprises (Ibrahim, Ebrashi, 2016). Those social enterprises that have chosen a nonprofit tax status will be especially impacted by the dynamic of volunteers, and the impact that they can have on the mission and functionality of the organization.

It is helpful for a social entrepreneur to be able to see any volunteers as another strata of the organizational stakeholders. These individuals have a stake in the organization, and it is imperative that the social entrepreneur engage them in such a way as to answer the question "How am I adding value to this group of stakeholders?" The ability of a manager, or leader, to effectively answer this question is vital to the overall ability of the volunteers or employees to be able to continue to support the overall mission of the organization.

Understanding the motivations of individuals is important when dealing with volunteers, as the motivation is not provided in the form of monetary remuneration, but must be the way the volunteer feels they're contributing to the overall goals of the mission. This focus on social value and return on investment is important for each volunteer and the effective social entrepreneur understands how to provide the most value for the time each volunteer spends contributing to the cause.

Research studies show that people are motivated by more than just money, and this is especially true of volunteers, who decide to give their time with no financial benefit, relying exclusively on the emotional social return on that time investment. In this way the effective entrepreneur must see volunteers, and in fact all employees, as stakeholders (Manetti, 2014). The manager should continue to find ways to add value to the exchange and to make sure that these individuals are getting the most out of their interaction and engagement with the enterprise.

Finding creative ways to help volunteers feel that they are not just contributing menial tasks but are in fact a vital part of the organization is an important role for any social entrepreneur or enterprise. By understanding each volunteer and what he or she desires to get out of the time commitment, the manager can effectively place them in positions where they will feel that their time is best spent and most in line with their individual values and goals. The manager can set up meetings to regularly check in with volunteers to see how they feel about the time they are spending contributing to the organization. This type of activity can help provide feedback and useful information to managers who oversee the activities of the volunteers.

Teams

Understanding the way in which individuals operate collectively is an important consideration in leveraging the skills and abilities of the volunteers or employees. There is no one person who can have all of the skills necessary for an organization to be successful at every possible aspect of the company. Therefore teams are created to help fill in skills gaps and to provide a multiplying factor for productivity and creativity.

However anytime there are teams or groups of individuals working together there must be effective communication and coordination of activities to ensure that the team dynamic is an asset to your organization and does not devolve into a liability. It is helpful to think of an organizational team like a football team, with different roles, skill sets, and positions working together to achieve a common purpose.

The effects of a team on an organization is a extensively studied phenomenon in organizational behavior. Teams, and the strengths and weaknesses of the individuals on the team, have an effect on the way in which each person works and sees his or her role in the organization. There are many ways that a social entrepreneur can leverage the effectiveness of teams in order to maximize their benefit to the organization.

Baldwin, Bommer, and Rubin (2013) list three ways in which teams can be most effectively utilized in an organization.

1. Teams can recommend things. For example, a team can be put together to do short-term research into a potentially new market and provide their recommendations to the management regarding whether or not a new venture will be worth the risk. These teams are typically short-term and have a specific start and end date.
2. Teams can make or do things. This type of team can be used to oversee a particular aspect of a company, especially as it relates to some of the most important and value-added aspects of the enterprise. These teams do not have specific start and end dates but instead are used to bring together multiple data inputs to be used to establish quality control of specific aspects of the company.
3. Teams can run things. Teams can be deployed in a management position as well, in order to run particular programs or activities in an enterprise. However, it is important for any manager or leader to remember that teams can be found at times to be preventive of direct and swift action, and this dynamic should be taken into account when determining whether or not a team is the most effective method of overseeing or running a portion of the organization.

This dynamic of swift action is especially important for early-stage social enterprises, as the ability to make quick decisions and respond immediately to unique challenges is important, and team operations may impede swift decision-making. This may not necessarily be a bad thing, but it should be taken into account by any social entrepreneur seeking to move forward quickly in the early stages of their endeavor. While multiple sources of information and opinion can help an entrepreneur to find a gaps in their thinking, or blind spots in their plans they didn't know existed, there is an aspect of diminishing returns when it comes to having too many influential voices speaking into the process.

Care2Rock

Care2Rock is an L3C based in Austin, Texas, that provides direct browser-to-browser music tutoring lessons to people across the country. Care2Rock founder, Karyn Scott, developed this idea while running her nonprofit, Kids in a New Groove (KING). KING provides one-on-one music mentoring to youth in the foster care system in the Austin area. Not only does this teach these kids musical skills, but it provides them with a supporting relationship that many in the foster care system desperately need. KING experienced great success locally, but Scott desired to extend their impact outside of central Texas. The technological advances in virtual communication allow Care2Rock to do this. The virtual lessons they provide can be accessed anywhere with an internet connection, and their tutors can conduct these lessons from anywhere in the country. Scott found that coordinating communication between tutors has been much easier than they expected and that many teachers are excited about the opportunity to teach online. However, the challenge is in getting the word out to their potential customer base. Scott believes that the social enterprise model is much more effective for creating change because it is scalable. However, she believes that if this is to be realized, more funding models need to be developed to support these businesses early.

©Africa Studio/Shutterstock.com

Virtual Teams

With the rise of effective and inexpensive virtual communication, it is more and more a realistic possibility for teams to operate and function in different geographic areas. **Virtual teams** can make use of many different methods including sharing documents, video conferencing, and email or chat communication.

> **Virtual Teams**
>
> A group of individuals who work together in an organization but do not meet or communicate in the same physical location.

This is an exciting new opportunity for social entrepreneurs as they are able to leverage the knowledge and skills of individuals all over the world. However, the virtual aspect of a team does affect the team dynamics and the ways in which they operate. These should be taken into account when assessing whether or not a virtual team will be the most productive means of accomplishing the task.

One positive aspect of virtual teams is that it allows for individuals with common characteristics and skills to be able to work toward a common goal regardless of time zone or geographic location (Kavoura & Anderson, 2016). This has the opportunity to create a diverse group of individuals who can effectively represent broad-based experiences to help the organization most effectively move forward.

A challenge of any team is to effectively establish trust in order to maximize the contributions of each individual. If the team members do not feel that they trust their teammates with their ideas then they may hold back, and the true potential of the team may not be realized (McShand & Von Glinow, 2015). It is therefore incumbent up on any manager or team leader to understand the challenge that can be present in establishing trust and communication and to take steps to build trust among the team members. Some team members may work better in a virtual capacity, while others may be a better fit with team members in the same geographic location, and the manager must be aware of this and choose the team members accordingly (McShand & Von Glinow, 2015). A culture of openness and trust is important especially in the presence of virtual teams.

How to Collaborate Effectively if Your Team is Remote

Communication today is becoming increasingly digital. While this is often a convenient and efficient way to transfer information, Dhawan and Chamorro-Premuzic (2018) observe that this brings several challenges to remote teams. They believe that a lack of the ability to use body language can cause messages to be misunderstood which can impact productivity, morale, and other factors that define a successful working environment. Similarly, they observe that digital communication is often not conducted at the same pace as physical communication. Lengthy response times can cause team members to become distracted and insecure, and, as a result, reduce their productivity. In order for remote teams to be successful, they must recognize these potential problems and develop appropriate guidelines that magnify the strengths of remote communication.

Dhawan and Chamorro-Premuzic (2018) identify five practices that can improve communication within remote teams. The first practice is to make each message as clear as possible. Often individuals believe a brief message will be efficient, but it is not if the recipient must spend time deciphering the true meaning behind the message. Similarly, it is important to respect individuals by considering the volume of messages sent to them. It can be very annoying to a coworker when they receive several follow-up emails before they get the chance to respond. The next practice is to develop norms for communication. This is important to do on a company-wide scale, such as requiring employees to include a desired response time on all messages. However, it is also important to recognize individual preferences, such as the amount of formality expected in an email. It is also important to acknowledge the advantages associated with remote communication. This includes using text-based communication to encourage introverted individuals to voice their opinion and reducing the chance of body language being misinterpreted. Lastly, it is important to celebrate milestones and accomplishments achieved by employees. Doing so can be difficult when team members are located across the country, but finding ways to celebrate with each other can greatly increase trust and camaraderie.

Conflict

Anytime a group of people interact over a period of time there is the opportunity for conflict to arise. It is incumbent upon the social entrepreneur to be able to navigate conflict effectively, knowing when it is appropriate and how to help it be constructive instead of destructive to the overall mission and vision of the organization.

Keashly & Nowell (2003) describe the conflict process and how individuals deal with conflict in a variety of ways. The way in which a person deals with conflict is due to a number of variables including personality and previous conflict resolution training and experience. Keashly & Nowell (2003) describe five ways in which individuals deal with conflict.

1. Problem-solving: This strategy represents a high concern for self and others. Through open exchange of information, common interests are identified to create integrative solutions meeting both parties' needs.
2. Obliging (accommodating, yielding): This strategy signifies a low concern for self but a high concern for others by emphasizing commonalties and downplaying differences.
3. Dominating (competing): Representing a high concern for self with low concern for others, this style focuses on fulfilling one's own interests at the expense of others.
4. Avoiding (withdrawing): This style represents a low concern for self and others. The objective is not to acknowledge or engage in the conflict situation.
5. Compromising: This involves an intermediate concern for self and others. By developing solutions that meet somewhere in the middle, both parties get some, but not complete, satisfaction. (p. 343)

Conflict in any organization can be a challenge and can present opportunities for a team to draw closer together or to move further apart. The successful social entrepreneur is able to help the team navigate the conflict in a healthy way.

It is also worth noting that not all conflict may take place between the individuals who are subordinate to the director or founding entrepreneur. There is also the potential for conflict between board members of a nonprofit company or between the board and the director of the nonprofit. For social entrepreneurs who desire to have a scalable and growing organization it is important for them to understand how to make conflict constructive and not destructive to the mission and vision of the organization.

This does not mean that all conflict is bad, on the contrary, some conflict is necessary and even helpful. Greenberg (2013) lists four ways in which conflict can be beneficial.

1. Conflict may improve the quality of organizational decisions.
2. Conflict may bring out into the open problems that have been previously ignored.
3. Conflict may motivate people to appreciate one another's positions more fully.
4. Conflict may encourage people to consider new ideas, thereby facilitating change. (p. 221)

It takes an intentional focus on creating a culture of constructive conflict to avoid the potentially mission-damaging effects of the natural tension that can exist between individuals.

Intrapreneurship

Not all innovation related to social enterprises takes place in a situation where an individual begins a new business venture and moves forward in a new organization. Some of the change agents begin to develop the concepts of social enterprise within an organization (Alt & Craig, 2016). These individuals who help to establish social innovation within an existing organization are intrapreneurs.

Grayson (2013) observed that organizational culture has an important effect on the ability for the social intrapreneur to be successful. Throughout his study, he interviewed twenty-five social intrapreneurs, and identified the following five key aspect of organizational culture as it relates to social intrapreneurship:

> **Organizational Culture**
>
> The formal and informal values that drive the behavior of individuals in an organization.

> **Intrapreneurship**
>
> The process of creatively seeking to use new methods or models to solve problems within an organization.

1. **Dialogue:** The ability for those within an organization to engage in open dialogue promotes the transfer and development of innovative ideas.
2. **Autonomy:** Creating an environment in which individuals are encouraged to develop ideas, instead of constantly having to fight against organizational structure, is essential to the intrapreneur's success.
3. **Risk-taking:** Intrapreneurial ideas do not come with a guarantee of success. For these ideas to be successful, the organization needs to encourage taking controlled risks and use failure as an opportunity for intrapreneurs to learn and grow.
4. **Experimentation:** Intrapreneurs need to be provided with the resources and support to experiment with new ideas.
5. **Sustainability:** The belief that success in business activities is directly related to developing responsible and sustainable business practices can foster long-term social intrapreneurship.

There are other factors that can either foster or obstruct social intrapreneurship, such as external connections with other organizations (suppliers, government agencies, etc.). These connections can help develop efficient plans and analyze the outcomes of intrapreneurial ideas, identify issues that need to be addressed in the industry, and communicate to stakeholders that their activities are making a difference. Also, connections between different departments within an organization can help identify different internal issues for intrapreneurs to observe.

Nonprofit and For-Profit Intrapreneurship

Kistruck (2010) identifies organizational form (nonprofit or for-profit), and structures (other legal formations that affect organizational actions) as other important factors for intrapreneurial success. Kistruck observed that nonprofits generally have a much harder time implementing social intrapreneurship than for-profits in developing countries. This is due, in part, to the cognitive, network, and cultural embeddedness, terms originating from Zukin and DiMaggio (1990), apparent within organizations.

Cognitive embeddedness refers to the mindset that is currently in place in the employees of a company. One of the major issues in integrating different forms on both sides, but especially from the position of the nonprofit, is changing the way individuals within the organization view budgets. One interviewee observed that, in general, when nonprofits receive donations, they do not think about the most profitable way to spend the money; rather they view it as an allotment of resources for a particular activity. This is very different from the for-profit business mindset and can be a very difficult shift for people who are used to operating under the nonprofit outlook. Also, balancing social and financial goals was a large issue, especially for nonprofit organizations. This is not only an issue with upper-level management, but also with lower-level employees. One interviewee observed that when employees were presented with materials from suppliers that were not up to their standards, those from a nonprofit background were likely to accept the materials if the supplier pleaded with them. Accepting these defective supplies contributed to low short- and long-term financial performance. On the other hand, employees from a for-profit background were more likely to reject the materials no matter how it would affect the supplier. Doing this allowed the organization to run more efficiently and better define the lines between their social and financial goals.

Network embeddedness refers to connections between different groups that cause dependencies between them. Before the study began, Kistruck believed that the ties between nonprofit organizations, operating in foreign countries, and their target groups would be a positive force when implementing more transactional-based activities. However, instead of supporting the traditionally goodwill-based organizations, many people within the target groups saw it as an opportunity to take advantage of them in the often ruthless markets. Also, the ties between nonprofit organizations and their funders were also hurt by the implementation of transactional approaches. These initiatives were often foreign to funders, and many were uneasy with the added factors of sustainability, middlemen, and government intervention. Similarly, entering and being sustainable in new markets proved to be very difficult for the nonprofit because of the lack of connections in the marketplace. However, for-profit organizations, who already have these connections in place, found it much easier to implement these socially driven initiatives. As a result, Kistruck discovered that one of the most important factors in developing healthy relationships with beneficiaries was to ensure that they were multidirectional from the start.

Cultural embeddedness refers to the overall beliefs of a group of people, not necessarily bound by geography, that govern an individual's view on suitable roles or actions. Kistruck found that trust is a large issue when trying to develop relationships with individuals in developing countries. One of the most helpful advantages to the nonprofit in developed countries is the general view people have of them as unselfish organizations, or organizations driven by a good cause. However, Kistruck found that this was not a sentiment shared by many individuals in developing countries. Most relationships were developed through past interactions and organizational reputation rather than institutional form. Similarly, another cultural challenge faced by nonprofit organizations is that most individuals in developing countries view nonprofits as strictly charitable and have become very reliant on the aid they provide. Rather than educating local populations on how to perform certain tasks, nonprofits have historically just done the work for them further cementing the unidirectional nature of their relationships. It can be very difficult for nonprofits to engage in social intrapreneurship when they are viewed in such a way. Although for-profits experience similar issues, they are not constrained to the extent that nonprofits are.

Mission Drift

Since social enterprises have both commercial revenue generation and social impact as core reasons for their existence, they face a unique challenge of balancing their efforts to achieve both financial and social goals. The risk social enterprises face of diverting more and more attention away from their social mission due to increased pressure to generate revenue is referred to

> **Mission Drift**
>
> The risk social enterprises face of diverting more and more attention away from their social mission due to increased pressure to generate revenue.

as mission drift. This happens naturally over time because appealing to the individuals or groups that purchase the social enterprise's products or services is necessary for sustainability, and without help from outside forces this can be very hard to avoid. Balancing these two aspects is not the only challenge social enterprises face. Social enterprises can have multiple principal stakeholders, including different beneficiaries and funders, and appealing to the interests of each one can often be a daunting task. Therefore, efficient organizational governance is essential for clearly defining which interests should be prioritized and for what, and to whom, the organization is accountable.

Ebrahim, Battilana & Mair (2014) identify two different types of social enterprises, integrated hybrids and differentiated hybrids, that experience mission drift in different ways. Integrated hybrids are organizations whose customers are the people who benefit from their products or services. Ebrahim, et al (2014) use VisionSpring to describe this model. VisionSpring produces eyeglasses and sunglasses to be sold in emerging markets using local organizations for distribution, and local women affected by poverty to sell the glasses in nearby villages. In this system, VisionSpring's beneficiaries (individuals in need of corrective lenses) are paying them directly. Conversely, differentiated hybrid's customers are independent of their beneficiaries. Ebrahim et al (2014) use Mobile School as an example for this system. Mobile

School provides corporate training programs to international and small corporations to generate revenue. They then use that revenue to provide mobile school carts to children free of charge. Differentiated hybrids experience mission drift when creating value for their customers begins to take precedence over creating value for their beneficiaries, causing them to divert resources away from their social mission and toward their commercial goals. Integrated hybrids experience mission drift when the organization prioritizes profits over providing their product or service to their beneficiaries for the best value. This may come in the form of price increases, shifts in customer base, profit focused product differentiation, etc.

Several different legal statuses for organizations have appeared over the last decade. One of these is the low-profit limited liability company (L3C) which allows the organization to structure their decision-making hierarchy in ways not available to the traditional LLC. This allows them to ensure that decisions are made by investors that are going to keep the social mission at the forefront of the organizations activities. Also, legislation usually requires the LLC to prioritize its social mission over its financial goals, but it does not dictate how the LLC is required to do this. The governing board is free to make these decisions on their own. Another legal form, the benefit corporation (B Corp), requires additional reporting and assessment of the social benefit of the corporation's actions, which is standardized by third-party organizations. However, there are few requirements place on the B Corp to prioritize their social mission. They simply need to apply the standards set by the third party to their organization. Ebrahim (2014) argues that while these statuses have helped reduce mission drift, they are unlikely to eliminate the risk completely. They help address external factors, but internal struggles to balance financial and social goals will still be present no matter what the legal status of the organization is Ebrahim also argues that monitoring the actions and performance of management, monitoring the interaction between commercial and social services, and implementing systems to maintain downward accountability to beneficiaries are all ways in which effective governance lessens the risk of mission drift.

Creating Organization Culture

The culture of an organization is a function of a number of factors, and it is different than the organizational strategy. There is the old adage that "culture eats strategy for breakfast" which gives an indication of the impact that organizational culture has on the long-term success of the business. In other words, the best strategy can't overcome a bad company culture.

When discussing culture it is primarily related to the "attitudes, values, behavioral norms, and expectations shared by members of an organization" (Greenberg, 2013). The culture that exists in an organization underpins the goals and strategy and can either be an asset to those goals or a liability. For example, if an organization desires to be a leader in innovation but does not have a culture that allows for the free flow of ideas due to fear of failure, it can undermine the goals of the organization.

One of the primary drivers of organizational culture is the attitude and behavior of the company founder, which is typically the entrepreneur who established the vision and mission of the company (Fauchart & Grube, 2011). This is an important factor for a social entrepreneur to understand, as they need to maintain a pulse on the culture of the organization, as it will reflect them and how they are able to both scale and someday potentially transition the organization to a new leader, which is a necessary component of a sustainable company. A sustainable company must be able to transition from founder to the next leader in a way that allows the culture and strategy to be maintained in a healthy way.

Conclusion

Social entrepreneurs rarely undertake new ventures alone. It is typically the efforts of a team or a group of stakeholders toward the common goal that characterizes effective social enterprises and social entrepreneurs. It is therefore important for new startups to understand the challenges and benefits that come along with both new and established organizations. Team dynamics as well as culture play a role in whether or not any social price can be successful, and paying attention to this important dynamic is in the best interest of any social startup.

References

Alt, E., & Craig, J. B. (2016). Selling Issues with Solutions: Igniting Social Intrapreneurship in for-Profit Organizations. Journal of Management Studies, 53(5), 794–820. https://doi.org/10.1111/joms.12200

Baldwin, Bommer, & Rubin (2013) *Managing Organizational Behavior: What Great Managers Know and Do*. New York: McGraw Hill.

Chang, Curtis. 2011. "Three Nonprofit Hiring Mistakes to Avoid." Stanford Social Innovation Review. https://ssir.org/articles/entry/three_nonprofit_hiring_mistakes_to_avoid

Davis, G. and White, C. (2015). Changing Your Company from the Inside Out: A Guide for Social Intrapreneurs. Boston, MA: Harvard Business Review Press.

Dhawan and Chamorro-Premuzic (2018) How to Collaborate Effectively if Your Team is Remote. https://hbr.org/2018/02/how-to-collaborate-effectively-if-your-team-is-remote?utm_camp aign=hbr&utm_source=facebook&utm_medium=social

Ebrahim, A., Battilana, J., & Mair, J. (2014). The governance of social enterprises: Mission drift and accountability challenges in hybrid organizations. *Research in Organizational Behavior, 34*(January 2016), 81–100. https://doi.org/10.1016/j.riob.2014.09.001

Fauchart, E., & Gruber, M. (2011). Darwinians, Communitarians, and Missionaries: The Role of Founder Identity in Entrepreneurship. The Academy of Management Journal, 54(5), 935–957. https://doi.org/10.5465/amj.2009.0211

Gordon, M. (2016). How social enterprises change: the perspective of the evolution of technology. *Journal of Social Entrepreneurship, 676*(January). https://doi.org/10.1080/19420676.2015.1086410

Grayson, P. D. (2013). Creating sustainable business through social intrapreneurship, (April), 1–40. Doughty Center for Corporate Responsibility.

Greenberg, J. (2013). *Managing Behavior in Organizations*, 6th edition. New Jersey: Pearson.

Grohs, S., Heinze, R. G., Schneiders, K., & De, R. H. (2017). Outsiders and Intrapreneurs: The Institutional Embeddedness of Social Entrepreneurship in Germany. *Voluntas: International Journal of Voluntary and Nonprofit Organizations, 28*, 2569–2591. https://doi.org/10.1007/s11266-016-9777-1

Ibrahim, S., & Ebrashi, R. El. (2017). How social entrepreneurship can be useful in long-term recovery following disasters. *Journal of Humanitarian Logistics and Supply Chain Management, 7*(3), 324–349. https://doi.org/10.1108/JHLSCM-04-2016-0009

Kavoura, A.; Andersson, T. (2016). Applying Delphi method for strategic design of social entrepreneurship. *Library Review*, *65*(3), 185–205.

Keashly, L., & Nowell, B. L. (2003). Conflict, conflict resolution and bullying. In S. Einarsen, H. Hoel, D. Zapf & C. L. Cooper (Eds.), Bullying and Emotional Abuse in the Workplace: International Perspectives in Research and Practice. (pp. 339–358). London, UK: Taylor & Francis.

Kistruck, G. M. and Beamish, P. (2010). The interplay of form, structure, and embeddedness in social intrapreneurship. *Entrepreneurship Theory and Practice*, *34*, 735–61.

Manetti, G. (2014). The role of blended value accounting in the evaluation of socio-economic impact of social enterprises. *Voluntas*, *25*(2), 443–464. https://doi.org/10.1007/s11266-012-9346-1

McShand & VonGlinow, 2015. Organizational Behavior. 7th edition. New York: McGraw-Hill.

Tan, W. L., Williams, J., & Tan, T. M. (2005). Defining the "social" in "social entrepreneurship": Altruism and entrepreneurship. *International Entrepreneurship and Management Journal*, *1*(3), 353–365. https://doi.org/10.1007/s11365-005-2600-x

Learning Outcomes

- Discover and recognize the components of organizational storytelling
- Apply storytelling to marketing and branding communication
- Synthesize information regarding personal and organizational branding for entrepreneurs
- Understand the importance of connection between audiences, organizations, communities, nonprofits and for-profits

Key Terms

Audience   Engagement
Backstory   Process
Brand   Storytelling
Character

RecycleForce

RecycleForce is a 501(c)(3) social enterprise that provides a wide range of recycling services to businesses, government agencies, municipalities, hospitals, universities, and reverse logistics providers in the Indianapolis area. A large portion of the materials RecycleForce processes are categorized as e-waste. These materials can have a lasting, detrimental effect on the environment and public health if they are not disposed of properly. RecycleForce has safely processed over 65 million pounds of these hazardous materials since 2006.

©weedezign/Shutterstock.com

Along with RecycleForce's mission to help create a cleaner environment, they also desire to break down barriers to employment through workforce training. They do this by providing six-month transitional jobs to individuals returning to society after serving time in prison. The rate that individuals return to the criminal justice system has been as high as 50% in the Indianapolis area. The jobs and services that RecycleForce provides are designed to help these people reintegrate into society and get their lives back on track. Since 2006, almost 1,200 men and women have gone through RecycleForce's program and have received on-the-job training as well as industry-recognized certifications. These services extend the effect RecycleForce has on these individuals past the six-month period they are with the organization by providing the skills and opportunities needed for full-time employment in the industry.

Founder of RecycleForce Gregg Keesling believes telling their story is the hardest thing RecycleForce does. People generally see them as a recycling business, a nonprofit trying to create a cleaner earth, or an organization trying to help formerly incarcerated individuals. However, people rarely see them as all three. For RecycleForce, trying to convey to the public, as well as to their employees, that they are a business with social issues at the core of their mission has been very difficult.

Storytelling

The act of explaining the concepts, beliefs, and values of a company or brand through stories, inviting the audience to recognize identifiable characters and empathize with their experiences. Stories acknowledge beliefs that are already in place, amplifying them with emotion and connection.

Storytelling is an ancient art, and while it may seem like a skill one is born with, this chapter will not only teach how to tell a story, but how to do it well. We also want to take it a step further and explain *why* stories resonate, especially in the arena of entrepreneurship. We listen to stories for multiple reasons, but one of the most powerful reasons is because stories do not directly tell us how to think and feel; thus, we welcome their points of view. Stories don't create our beliefs; rather, their themes draw us in and bring us close to what we already believe, and they give us a place to change our minds without censure.

A simple definition of story does not truly exist. The Merriam-Webster Dictionary defines story as "an account of incidents or events" or "a fictional narrative shorter than a novel." Walter Fisher, author of *Human Communication as Narration*, posits that humans are storytelling animals, that we cannot escape the power of story because our communication is almost all fundamentally narrative.

Telling a story is translating an experience into something that we can think about or pass on to others; it is a type of narration. Vacation pics on Instagram? That's storytelling. Blogging about your idea for a Cuban food truck? That's storytelling. This fundamental desire to tell stories is innate, and as individuals share something from past and even present experience, they engage an audience, who either buys in or doesn't, but the story cannot be ignored. Because we, as humans live in stories, we cannot dismiss the importance they hold.

Audience

The potential customers and supporters of a company, brand, or product, toward whom the brand story is aimed or crafted.

Brand

The name, term, sign, symbol, or design, or any combination of the previous, intended to identify the goods and services of one seller or group of sellers and to differentiate them from those of other sellers.

Storytelling is not limited to marketing or advertising—it's a fundamental area for all aspects of communication, especially for entrepreneurs. From the PR perspective of branding and digital communication, storytelling allows audiences to share their stories in ways that interweave into the larger fabric of a community or brand's story. Storytelling, especially digital storytelling, functions strategically to integrate multiple stories and viewpoints, giving voice not only to individual identities, but creating a larger, communal brand identity.

Community connection drives the most powerful and dynamic story a brand can tell—a brand's reputation. And reputation is formed by the *perceptions* of a brand—perceptions that arise from audiences, whether internal or external, public or private, shareholder or client. Community connection comes from understanding an audience and giving them opportunities for two-way engagement. Engaging with a brand, organization, and/or other members of an audience is what drives connection and interaction.

Engagement and the resulting audience response allows practitioners to execute effective campaign tactics and programming to meet objectives. This chapter will move through the importance of the process of entrepreneurial storytelling, by extending Signorelli's (2014) concept of StoryBranding to community connection and audience understanding through digital storytelling, where public relations practitioners can engage audiences, execute creative programming, meet objectives, and provide space for a shared sense of meaning to emerge.

Trust the Process

A good story follows standards of form and function. Stories have character. Stories have conflict. Stories have a plot. There's a protagonist. There's a battle to overcome. Think of these pieces as ingredients; separately we know what they are, how to find them, and that without one of them, the dish won't be complete. But the most important thing is connection with the audience.

Separately each item/ingredient is checked off the list, but then the key step—blending the ingredients. And now the dish starts to come together. This is why not everyone is a gifted storyteller. Or cook. It's the planning that makes the dish great—a recipe if you will—and it needs to be understood. A great story is no different. There's a plan and a process.

The process of storytelling will yield solid connection and understanding between the writer or creator and the reader or audience. So, let's figure out how to take simple steps and turn it into your story, *your* organization's story, one that resonates both internally and externally.

The key to understanding process and story is realizing it takes time. Telling an important story requires time to flow smoothly and have the impact desired. Three things come into play in the early stages of the process; concept or goal, characters, and audience relationship.

Concept & Backstory

Concepts are not ideas. Ideas are too small. Concepts need history or a backstory. How did the situation or context originate? In traditional marketing parlance, this is often referred to as the situation analysis (Signorelli, 2014). It is important to understand the place of the company in the marketplace—think origination stories. SheaMoisture has a great origin story and it is on every product they sell, whether packaging or label.

Engagement

The process of forming an emotional or rational attachment between a consumer and a brand; it is most well recognized in marketing terms as brand engagement or customer engagement.

Process

A series of actions or steps taken in order to achieve a particular end. In the storytelling and branding process, process is a systematic approach used to create, communicate, and strengthen a firm's brand. It consists of a number of sequential steps. These steps may vary depending on who is implementing the process and the specific outcomes the firm is trying to achieve.

Character

The main people in a story—here the brand or the customer—that have the greatest effect on the plot or are the most affected by the events of the story; they are relatable, take action, and have articulated goals.

Backstory

The history of a company or creator, offering the reason for product creation or a company coming into existence; the "why" behind the current company or product.

Sofi Tucker started selling Shea Nuts at the village market in Bonthe, Sierra Leone in 1912. By age 19, the widowed mother of four was selling Shea Butter, African Black Soap and her homemade hair and skin preparations all over the countryside. Sofi Tucker was our Grandmother and SheaMoisture is her legacy. (www.sheamoisture.com)

Backstories provide a foundation, a platform. Concepts are platforms from which a story can unfold. In *StoryBranding 2.0*, Jim Signorelli makes the point that obstacles are required for great stories. They need to be confronted. By categorizing the obstacles that the brand must deal with, an organization is able to move strategically and thoughtfully toward its goals.

Characters

People are multidimensional; and so should the brand characters be. They are the layers of flavor in the dish. Think of texture, taste, and appearance. Characters can be easy to physically describe, but that is merely the exterior layer, or appearance. Dig deeper to reveal their habits, their vices, and their strengths. Characters should have multiple layers with articulated worldviews and frames of reference. In marketing terms, Signorelli calls this description and understanding characterizing the brand (2014). Best understood as investigation of the brand and an understanding of the brand's value and belief system, those beliefs must be supported throughout cohesive communication.

Signorelli encourages research in being able to accurately characterize the Prospect, or target audience (2014). This is done through research and exploration of the client or prospect's needs, desires, or functional opportunities. Qualitative data here is key; whether through surveys, focus groups, or individual interviews, enterprises need the "why."

For these two "characters"—the brand and the prospect/client—to truly blend, a strong connection needs to be articulated and established. This connection goes beyond form and function. For example, someone needs to purchase a wallet to hold money and cards—there are many brands that can service that need, functioning to hold money and cards well. But enterprises and brands need to move beyond satisfying the functional—they need relationship.

Relationship

Marketers and advertisers are working to create relationship between brand and client, with the story, a resonance, or shared understanding, such as a "You too? I thought I was the only one!" moment, empathy for the plight of the ones who need saving, or a shared desire for victory. An audience needs to *feel* something for the story to live on, to be told and retold. A question an entrepreneur needs to ask is, "How do I do this for a business?" For example, a small business owner asks, "How do I create relationship between a brand and client for a small town printing service?" One answer is a unique value proposition, or UVP.

Coined by Signorelli, UVP is the unique belief that a brand hopes both employees and prospects associate with the brand beyond its functional purpose (2014). A brand's UVP truly has nothing to do with form, function, or benefit, but instead its goal is to articulate what a brand believes and values. A good UVP extols a belief, not a benefit. Consider the small town printing service; yes, they need to do their job well (benefit), but that is not what creates relationship. Relationship is built when clients recognize the owner's commitment to integrity and how they help serve low-income kids in the local community (belief).

Personal Story Branding

These three fundamental pieces of storytelling—process, backstory, and characters—might seem simplistic, but to execute them well requires thoughtfulness and creative thinking. Practicing these steps is easiest when there is familiarity with the company, organization, or person being "branded." The initial directive, then, as the entrepreneur, is to get familiar with the company story.

Making the story applicable and practical requires that you connect and engage with your entrepreneurial side. How does your story translate into the marketplace? What kind of business suits you best and what kind of business needs you and your story? Prior to crafting and executing the story of a business you work for or have created, you need to have a solid grasp on the questions (and answers) regarding your own brand. The questions below are created first and foremost for the entrepreneur, but using a personal focus first creates space to play with story.

Questions to Think About

1. Identify your personal brand. What are your values? What do you stand for?
2. Are your current activities/marketing messages in alignment with your brand values?
3. Are you trying to be all things to all people? In what areas are you stretching to do something that is outside your expertise or ability? Is that benefiting or harming your customers?
4. Characterize your ideal target audience. What are their demographics and their values and beliefs?
5. Are *my* values and *my* message in alignment with those of my prospects/clients?
6. Identify your unique value proposition. What belief do you want people to identify with your brand?
7. Consider how you tell your story. Are you focused on Big-T truths (feelings and emotions) or on small-t truths (facts and features)? How could you rewrite your brand story to be more effective?

An entrepreneur and their business enterprise cannot be all things to all people, but it is possible to figure out the best fit and where each business can flourish. The key is finding the place where ideas have traction and people are onboard and supportive—this is organizational community. How does storytelling fit into the community setting?

Storytelling that Resonates

Communities are becoming progressively defined by the personal stories shared by community members instead of the community's larger brand narrative. Why are these individual stories, histories, and experiences able to garner such attention? How can sharing an experience through social media cause community growth, social consciousness, or even new communities to emerge? The answer to both questions is digital storytelling: using multimedia outlets to share stories creates spaces for education, social change and reflection. Available to entrepreneurs and organizations alike, digital storytelling creates connections, bolsters brand identity, empowers expression, and expands personal voice.

How can one engage digital storytelling in ways that are compelling and effective? By understanding what storytelling is and what it can do. Not only do stories resonate with us as Fisher's explanation of "storytelling animals," but the structure of digital storytelling aligns with the way we learn, aiding in memorization and recall, and resonating in a way that mere facts cannot. Stories are vessels, creating a sense of life and color. The medium through which these stories are shared is often described as "the message," and that rings true here as well; multimedia has revolutionized storytelling.

There are certain requirements for a good story—conflict, characters, backstory, resolution—but perhaps the most important requirement is for the story to resonate with the audience. When an organization fails to listen to their consumers or audience, when companies forget what their audience values, stories fail. "My" story needs to connect to "your" story to create an "our" story. Just as an excellent storyteller ("me") anticipates what the audience ("you") wants, PR practitioners must consider how the audience thinks—there is no room for disconnect between audience and storyteller—and they must create a shared meaning, a shared "our" story that, in turn, creates a larger brand narrative, or the shared reputation.

Stories must also be shaped to fit the self-conception of a specific audience. "Any story, any form of rhetorical communication," Fisher writes, "not only says something about the world, it also implies an audience, persons who conceive of themselves in very specific ways" (1984). Understanding this conception of self, or frame of reference, is how we make brand messaging resonate with selected target audiences.

Framing the Message

Sweetland (2018) describes framing for social issues as "mosaics, constructed bit by bit through the many decisions advocates make whenever they write an email blast, send out a press release, give an interview, or present to a group." One element that cannot be overlooked is the *nature* of the storyteller. Audiences may discredit the opinions of a speaker or author if they do not believe they are trustworthy or unbiased, regardless of the message or story. Thus, it is important to recognize the perception of the speaker, by the audience. Another important area to consider is the *tone* of the message being delivered.

Knowing the audience is *essential* for storytellers. For example, if the purpose of telling the story of an organization's history is to create interest around a certain issue within a group, a more explanatory tone will likely improve the audience's perception of the information. On the other hand, messages with strong and controversial wording can create further separation between the messenger and audience. The goal is connection, not separation.

Community Connection

Good storytelling is highly descriptive. It brings people together. Communication in the narrative enables us to share our understandings of how the world works and allows us to identify with one another, particular if we are party to similar beliefs. Fisher's narrative paradigm demonstrates that our attitudes can be directed by story and can move us to sympathy. Fisher recognizes that to some degree we have a desire for drama. Combined with our quickness to pass judgment when we can identify with a story, narrative is an incredibly effective form of rhetoric as both a communicative technique and a persuasive tool. It helps us to create meaning and connect with others. We can use it to consider moral constructs and increase our knowledge of any situation.

From the PR perspective of StoryBranding, storytelling allows audiences to share their stories in ways that interweave into the larger fabric of a community or brand's story. The work of Lambert and Miller explains that digital storytelling functions strategically to integrate multiple stories and viewpoints and give voice not only to individual identities, but to create a larger communal brand identity. This cohesive voice, the communal brand identity, drives the most powerful and dynamic story a brand can tell: a brand's reputation. Understanding an audience and giving them opportunities for two-way engagement with a brand, organization, or other members of that audience drives connections and interaction. Engagement and the resulting audience response allows practitioners to execute effective campaign tactics and programming to meet objectives. This project hopes to demonstrate that by extending Signorelli's concept of StoryBranding to digital storytelling, public relations practitioners can engage audiences, execute creative programming, meet objectives, and provide space for a shared sense of meaning to emerge.

Lambert, alongside Dana Atchley, established the Center for Digital Storytelling in 1993 to "support individuals and organizations in using storytelling and participatory media for reflection, education, and social change" (storycenter.org). Lambert and Atchley's creative strategy, called "Seven Elements of Digital Storytelling," has been used by educators, local governments, social and healthcare centers, and more recently, organizations and businesses to connect individuals and societies via shared stories. Their multilayered approach provides support for how an individual can reflect on personal experiences that can be (1) shared with others, (2) interpreted, evaluated, and/or analyzed, (3) used to persuade belief and/or action, and (4) formed into a co-constructed identity. Ultimately, these shared stories can prompt engagement, action, and the emergence of a shared sense of meaning rooted in understanding and celebrating difference.

Beyond the technique of telling a story, the ethical and philosophical aspects are pivotal to prosperous public relations, and although individuals tell their stories, it is the public relation practitioners who communicate or narrate their connections. This practice produces two-way dialogue, the give-and-take between listener and teller, the goals of which are mutual understanding and mutual respect (Gruing & Hunt, 1994; Lattimore, Baskin, Heiman, and Toth, 2011). This storytelling practice also unites individuals and communities through the sharing of human struggles and confrontation of common challenges, thus enhancing and enriching social capital (Putnam, 2001). Barbara Ganley writes:

> A healthy community—no matter the setting—is grounded in belonging, in understanding, in plurality. … When relationships are built and strengthened through deep storytelling, people feel welcomed and valued, and civic participation is enhanced. Just as in the classroom. People feel better about their communities. And positive change can follow (qtd. in Lambert, 2013).

Reflected in current marketplace trends at both individual and organizational levels, the digital storytelling initiative enables public relations practitioners and scholars to initiate and invite dialogue, draw connections between ideas and actions, and ultimately bridge the gap between individuals and communities.

Lambert's *Digital Storytelling: Capturing Lives, Creating Community* demonstrates digital storytelling's many unique roles, promoting positive ways to tackle uncertainty and doubt in an ever-changing landscape. As a learning community, digital storytelling advocates for the revitalization of shared spaces. As an agent for social change, digital storytelling builds a culture of inclusion while it aids in conflict resolution and negotiation. Looking at storytelling from a public relations standpoint allows us to demonstrate rich opportunities to engage stakeholders, cultivate relationships, build or rebuild communities, and respond to difference in ways that are compelling and meaningful.

The Process of Story Crafting

Stories can be incorporated into all forms of content: blogs, e-books, whitepapers, and even your "About Us" page to captivate the target audience. The value of storytelling can also be transferred to other departments to grow a business, such as training sales representatives to tell the backstory of the company or telling the entrepreneur's personal, founding story to captivate investors and donors. An effective and compelling story will produce an audience that desires to hear more, turning readers and hearers into leads, leads into customers, and customers into brand loyal customers.

Below are some foundational questions to help entrepreneurs craft their story and know when to tell it. The sections below list practical questions to ask, think about, research and answer, so that the story is successful, authentic and compelling.

What Really Matters?

1. Don't start at the very beginning, unless it's crucial. Start where the action is. Pick three things to share and stop there. Don't share too much information, especially useless details. No one cares that it was midnight instead of 11:30 p.m. Details eat into the flow. Strategically releasing pertinent information, arouses curiosity. Curiosity is important. A storyteller hopes for an audience to say, "Keep going. Then what happened?"

2. Relate to your audience by sharing. Joyce Meyer has a saying, "your mess is your ministry" and Bates (2016) states that, "people relate to your mess, not your success." Pride has no place in getting people to get on board. Engage people where they are. If social change and community building is a goal of your storytelling, then you need to be on that level.

3. Remember that emotion and the senses have an important role for connection. Engage the senses, describe things, help the audience feel as if they are there on the battlefield. A terrific example of this is Denzel Washington's challenge at Gettysburg, to his football team in *Remember the Titans*. Simply put, if your audience doesn't feel anything, they won't remember anything.

What Kind of Stories Should I Tell?

It helps to think of communication as a kind of toolbox; it can be dramatic and persuasive, planned and detailed, or directed and compelling. Similarly, there are many kinds of stories that can be told to convey a point, elicit a response, or make the unexplainable understandable.

Why Are We Here? Stories

Transparency is key when answering the question, "why?" You need to inform listeners of your intentions up front and create trust. Many clients and customers are more receptive if you simply tell them you are selling a product/service at the beginning of the pitch.

Vision-Casting and Goal-Setting Stories

Communicate your vision and inspire others to act. For example, you could relay a story about how a product or service saved a company. Or, perhaps a company folded because decision-makers didn't act quickly enough. Think about a company requiring a cultural change. We need to make it easier for management to embody the new story and to convey the message to the broader organization. So instead of planning typical roadshows to cascade the new (improved) message, we gather with the management to translate the abstract and rational message into real, emotional stories that are recognizable to employees.

Who Am I? Stories

Demonstrate who you are, and who the company is, to people and create a connection to your beliefs and values. It's more than what someone is selling, it's about the UVP—the beliefs, values, and the process that made you who you are today.

Company Backstories

History is important. How did you, as an entrepreneur, get your start? Why a food truck? Why did you use the graphic of an open book as the logo? Share that background knowledge and inform others of the company history. This gives listeners something they have not heard or considered. In the context of a story, listeners then remember *your* story and history.

It is imperative to note that these historical stories are not created; they are and have been lived. For example, during a branding retreat, a consultant might gather together core members of the company for a 'story session'; the consultant would then ask them to identify concrete events in the company's past that are actually good illustrations of what the future should look like. Find examples of employees, management, and stockholders that highlight the attitudes, values, and beliefs that the new messaging/branding embodies, then craft the story the company moves forward with, to perhaps drive a new initiative.

Obviously, there could be many other events and practices from clients' or a company's past that would be no longer in line with the new strategy. These are stories that need to be forgotten. Think about creating a timeline for the company for the process of storytelling. Reflect on which of these stories can serve as inspiration for the future and which ones should become past tense. This is actually no different from the parables in the Bible or origin stories in other cultures; the selected stories become symbols and touchstones guiding or inspiring behavior in future challenges.

When to Use Stories?

In order for a story to be truly effective, the timing must be on point. It is a lot like a joke; told well, laughter opens up a conversation and a sense of camaraderie, but misjudged, it causes awkwardness. Similarly, a misplaced story seems forced, and can fall flat. PowerPoints or corporate talks simply do not have a viral effect. Stories do. Below you will find recommendations for when story is most appropriate:

1. When you need to create buy-in: This may be best known as "vision-casting." When well-crafted, vision-casting can be extremely effective. In the past, stories have been known to start entire social and political movements by creating such a personal connection that people need to be a part of it.

2. When you are pitching or presenting: Raw data is almost impossible to remember, but it is important. Stories within presentations offset this and accomplish more than one simple thing; they make facts memorable, grab your attention, and make data understandable and something the audience can relate to.

3. When you are selling a product or service: Tell, don't sell. However, telling sales stories can convey the true power of your product or service. In a story, you provide context to customers and can drive points home harder. Use your own actual experiences or those of your company. Third party stories have little to no value.

4. When you are introducing yourself/company: It is difficult to remember names, backgrounds, resumes, and plans. Tie those things to a story, and you remember not only the person, but you learn who they are and what they can bring to the proverbial table.

People often refute that business should not be about stories but about facts and figures, about rational analysis and objectivity, rather than about emotions and subjectivity; perhaps it should be when it comes to making important decisions. But once decisions are discussed and made, the biggest challenge often lies in changing the mindsets of people affected, to adhere to the decision, to igniting the action that is needed to implement the decision and contribute to its successful rollout.

Storytelling is a highly effective tool to tackle those challenges, because our brains were built this way. Research shows that storytelling evokes a strong neurological response (Zak, 2015). Our brain produces the stress hormone cortisol during the tense moment in a story, which allows us to focus, while the human, emotional factor releases oxytocin, the feel-good chemical that promotes connection and empathy. Other neurological research teaches us that a happy ending to a story triggers the limbic system to release dopamine which makes us feel more hopeful and optimistic (Zak, 2015).

This physical, neurological response to story is compelling and should be understood. Just as the process of developing a story is one of discovery, of guiding principles, of trial and error, so is the world of social entrepreneurship. When someone has a question or sees a need within the community, they test it, ask questions, try programs, do research, and draw conclusions. Experimenting with business and attaching social cause is a fact-finding mission. What works? What audience do we need to reach? How can they best be served by our business? Answering these questions is not easy, but it is necessary and it is part of the process.

The process of creating anything worthwhile is labor intensive, and requires balance. The over-planner may never actually get to starting the business. The ones who act too quickly are often over-zealous but have no staying power. Storytelling, done well, is balanced; balance between emotion and data, facts and compassion, history and vision. Start the process, work well, and work thoroughly, plan for alternatives and consider all possible outcomes, targets, critiques. Understand who the audience is, what they need to hear, what you need to say and how best to say it.

References

Bates, J. (2016). John Bates: Success Stories from Coaching Hundreds of TEDx Talks. Fri, 09 Sep 2016 http://www.timetoshinepodcast.com/john-bates-success-stories-coaching-hundreds-tedx-talks/. Accessed July 2018.

Fisher, W. (1987). Human Communication as Narration: Toward a Philosophy of Reason, Value, and Action. Columbia, SC: University of South Carolina Press.

Fisher, W. R. (1984) Narration as a human communication paradigm: The case of public moral argument, Communication Monographs, 51:1, 1–22, DOI: 10.1080/03637758409390180

Grunig, J. E. and T. Hunt. (1994). Public Relations Techniques. Fort Worth, TX: Harcourt College Publishers.

Grunig, J. E. (2013). Excellence in Public Relations and Communication Management. Abingdon, UK: Routledge.

Lambert, J. (2012). Digital Storytelling: Capturing Lives, Creating Community (Digital Imaging and Computer Vision) 4th Edition. Abingdon, UK: Routledge.

Lattimore, D., Baskin, O., Heiman, S., and Toth, E. (2011). Public Relations: The Profession and Practice. New York McGraw-Hill.

Meyer, J. Let your mess become your message. https://joycemeyer.org/dailydevo/2018/06/0630-let-your-mess-become-your-message. Accessed July 2018.

Putnam, R. (2001). Bowling Alone: The Collapse and Revival of American Community. New York: Simon & Schuster.

SheaMoisture. https://www.sheamoisture.com/our-story/ Accessed July 2018.

Signorelli, J. (2014). StoryBranding 2.0: Creating Standout Brands Through the Purpose of Story. 2nd Edition. Chicago: Story-Lab Publications.

Sweetland, J. (2018, February 28). What's in a Frame? A Need to Know for Nonprofits. Retrieved April 11, 2018, from https://nonprofitquarterly.org/2018/02/27/whats-frame-heres-nonprofit-advocates-need-know In an effort to make these choices clearer for those in the social sector, the FrameWorks Institute has developed a list of "frame elements" communicators must consider: (http://www.frameworksinstitute.org/assets/files/PDF/comms_jobs.pdf).

Zak, P. J. (2015). Why Inspiring Stories Make Us React: The Neuroscience of Narrative. Cerebrum: The Dana Forum on Brain Science, 2015, 2. Accessed July 2018.

PART 4:

Financing

Chapter 9:

Start-up Financing and Scaling

Learning Outcomes

- Compare various methods of start-up financing
- Examine the dual aspects of financial and social scaling
- Explain common start-up methods
- Assess the ethical issues associated with fundraising

Key Terms

Bootstrapping	Lean Start-up
Distributed Ledger	Microfinance
Fundraising	Scaling Impact

Start-up Financing

There are a number of ways that businesses and organizations can gain the investment needed to begin and to scale. This chapter will look at some of the options available to social entrepreneurs to help them get off the ground, as well as the potential issues associated with scaling.

The method of financing may be impacted based on the tax status and revenue model that has been identified as most viable for the company. For example, if a company decides that a non-profit status will provide the best method for generating revenue and the best organizational mission, then the manner in which the organization gains start-up capital will be different, as it will

> ### Fundraising
>
> The organized activity for raising funds. It can take on a number of different forms, including dinner events, auctions, or soliciting donors for money.

likely take on a more traditional **fundraising** model. However, if the company has decided that a for-profit model provides the most options for revenue and scalability, then the start-up financing may take the form of more traditional loans and the pitching of ideas to investors.

The key is to maintain alignment between the organizational mission, model, and methods for financing and scalability. This chapter will look at a few of the options available.

Lean Start-up

According to the US Bureau of Labor Statistics, approximately half of all new businesses don't survive past their fifth year. There are many viewpoints regarding why this is a reality, and equally as many opinions on how to most effectively start a

A start-up that trades traditional straight-line product development for a more agile approach with a focus on customer development.

lasting business. One of these methods that has been generating attention over the last several years is called the lean start-up. The lean start-up trades traditional straight-line product development for a more agile approach with a focus on customer development (Blank, 2013). Blank observed three characteristics of start-ups that followed the traditional business plan development structure. First, a start-up's first interaction with customers frequently derails business plans. Second, start-ups that attempt to forecast long term unknowns are generally unsuccessful and end up wasting a lot of time and resources trying to do so. Third, start-ups do not develop the same way as large companies. They achieve success by quickly learning from their mistakes and adapting their products to customer feedback.

In response to these factors, Blank discourages the creation of elaborate business plans and instead encourages development of a "business model canvas." The business model canvas is a framework for clearly communicating how a product or idea adds value to the consumer and the start-up itself. It accomplishes this by outlining each segment of the organization's structure from key partners, activities, and resources, to value propositions, and distribution channels. A detail video describing this process can be found at https://hbr.org/video/2363593484001/sketch-out-your-hypothesis.

As mentioned previously, Blank (2013) observes that the lean start-up focuses on gathering information from consumers about the different aspects of their business model. This includes their pricing strategy, product characteristics and features, and more. Once the feedback has been received, changes to the product or business model are made and more information is gathered. This cycle is referred to as customer development. The success of a customer development approach is predicated on speed and flexibility so that bad ideas can be weeded out quickly and good ideas can be identified and implemented. This iterative process is also referred to as agile development. Product developers create what is referred to as a minimum viable product which contains only critical features. New minimum viable products are then formed from customer feedback, and the process starts over again. This process saves the start-up time and resources by making target changes based on the factors customers find most important, as opposed to traditional methods of product development, which make assumptions about these variables (Blank, 2013).

Bootstrapping

A variety of nontraditional techniques used by entrepreneurs to generate startup funding and/or reduce the costs associated with starting a business.

Bootstrapping

Bootstrapping refers to a variety of nontraditional techniques used by entrepreneurs to generate start-up funding and/or reduce the costs associated with starting a business. Specifically, this means reducing or eliminating the reliance on long-term financing from external sources. Instead, funds are raised/saved in the form of loans from family and friends, purchasing/renting used equipment, and a number of other unique methods (Perry, Chandler, Yao, and Wolff, 2011). Although these techniques are often a response to the scarcity of resources available to new ventures, firms that do have access to these resources also use bootstrapping as a strategic means for retaining control of their organization.

There are differing opinions within the academic community regarding the viability of bootstrapping techniques. On one hand, many scholars believe they can increase the profitability of the firm by allowing business owners to manage their cash more efficiently. However, others believe that taking this route adversely affects the firm in the long-term by reducing its ability to secure traditional investment funding later in its life cycle. Similarly, there is a belief that the large portion of time firms are required to focus on developing and maintaining these methods could be better spent on tasks that are more crucial to the new venture's growth and sustainability (Ye, 2017). Despite these differences in opinion, Lahm and Little (2005) observe that a large number of entrepreneurial start-ups are using bootstrapping methods in some capacity. However, they note that the number of businesses that rely solely on this form of funding is difficult to quantify. Lahm and Little also recognize that, despite the outcome of implementation, individuals who are forced to adopt practices often develop unique skills that those with access to a readily available pool of resources often lack. Specifically, these individuals need to learn how to be resourceful in their managerial and entrepreneurial practices.

Although the market for external financing for social enterprises has grown in recent years, many new businesses find it difficult to secure adequate funding for their operations due to a variety of different issues. This includes factors such as information asymmetries, agency theory, and transaction costs (Cassar, 2004). Business financing decisions must be made carefully as they have been shown to affect business operations, risk, performance, and expansion potential (Cassar, 2004).

Foundations

The origins of charitable foundations are debated, but it is clear that they have grown into an incredibly large institution in many developed economies today (Anheier and Leat, 2014). According to the Foundation Center (2013), at the start of 2014 there were over 86,000 independent, corporate, community, and operating foundations in the US alone. These organizations owned a fair market value of assets totaling over $865 billion. Although the expansion of philanthropic institutions has been clear over the last couple decades, Anheier and Leat (2014) observe that there has been little discussion over the role and rationale for them in their host societies. However, they note that the literature that does exist on this topic contains several common themes. These themes include that they are important in society but are often limited in their impact; they are often seen as supplementary to government; that their existence in democratic societies seems abnormal; and that their function is still not completely established, preventing them from realizing their full potential.

Explanations for the continuous existence of foundations are varied. However, Anheier and Leat believe that a straightforward explanation for this is that society perceives them as valuable. They observe that although society has historically been very accepting of foundations and what they wish to accomplish, they are not free of skepticism. A common argument against their existence is that they are an unsuitable way for the elite, who often create these foundations to impact public policy through the use of private funds. Many believe this is not appropriate in a democratic environment. Similarly, foundations can also be seen as a way for the country's elite to improve their public image. This is not, in itself, a bad thing. However in some cases, critics believe this money could be more impactful if it were used to improve working conditions within the foundation founder's company.

Despite the many criticisms of foundations, they continue to exist and flourish in the US and abroad. Anheier and Leat state that the reason for their generally positive public perception is likely a combination of several factors. This includes the fact that there is little urgency from politicians to develop substitutes for the foundation model and the view individuals generally have that they are harmless to society. However, Anheier and Leat argue that any argument in favor of foundations must be supported with evidence that the societal contributions of the foundation are larger than the costs. This is of particular importance because part of a foundation's impact is generated by taxpayers. Porter and Kramer (1999) state that although foundations can leverage their very large tax and administrative costs to create social value, they can be very inefficient if not held to the proper standards.

Lenders

Banks

The traditional lending method would look something like a loan from a bank in order to pursue capital investments for growth for the company. This method is typically associated with for-profits. However, a nonprofit that has shown revenue generation capabilities may also be an option for a lender. The bottom line is that the organization must establish a reliable method of revenue so that the loan may be paid back with interest.

Community Development Finance Institutions

According to the Community Development Finance Institution Fund (CDFI Fund), CDFIs are organizations that seek to provide economic opportunities for individuals in low-income communities. They do this by providing businesses and community residents with easily accessible financial products and services. Today CDFIs exist across the United States in the form of credit unions, banks, loan funds, microloan funds, and venture capital providers. The CDFI Fund was created by the Riegle Community Development and Regulatory Improvement Act of 1994 with the purpose of supporting CDFIs through investments and various others forms of assistance (https://www.cdfifund.gov/Documents/CDFI_infographic_v08A.pdf).

Appleyard (2011) studies the financial exclusion of enterprises through analysis of CDFIs in the US and the UK. She observed that CDFIs have been successful in providing funding for many financially excluded enterprises, but they still leave many geographical gaps of financial exclusion. This is due, in part, to their approach in dealing with this issue. For example, UK based CDFIs are considered "lenders of last resort." This means that if a business wants to receive an investment from the CDFI, they must provide proof of rejection from mainstream financial institutions. However, US-based CDFIs do not have this requirement. Appleyard observed that this puts US CDFIs in direct competition with mainstream banks, which often drives the focus of the CDFI away from their social mission in favor of achieving their economic objectives. US CDFIs are therefore more likely to focus their investments in less risky areas rather than the areas that need the most help. Appleyard suggests that, in this context, UK CDFIs are positioned better for tackling the problem of financial exclusion in their communities.

Microfinance Institutions

As mentioned in Chapter 1, microlending, or microfinance, refers to the provision of small loans to businesses or individuals for the purpose of alleviating poverty. Microfinance Institutions (MFIs) serve as centers for administering these loans and for providing educational resources and support for the recipients, who are often in developing countries. Ideally, this process provides businesses with the resources they need to become sustainable and, as a result, bolsters the local economy from the bottom up. However, the role of MFIs is debated from two opposing viewpoints, the institutionalist approach and the welfarist approach (Woller, 1999). According the institutionalist approach, the MFI should be primarily focused on internal financial sustainability and scaling. On the other hand, the welfarist approach claims that the MFI should emphasize an outward focus on direct social performance. Bos and Millone (2012) observe that this debate is primarily centered around a disagreement about how MFIs can most efficiently function. A consensus concerning exactly what composes functional efficiency has yet to be developed in the microfinance field.

> **Microfinance**
>
> The provision of small loans to businesses or individuals for the purpose of alleviating poverty.

Perhaps the most influential factor in this debate is whether or not a trade-off between social and financial sustainability can realistically exist within MFIs. Schreiner (2002) lays out the following six aspects of social impact realization in microfinance:

1. **Worth** refers to a client's "willingness to pay." Schreiner gives the example of a farmer who needs $1,000 to drill a well. For this client, a loan of $100 has little worth because it does not fulfil his demand. However, the client is not the only beneficiary of microfinance. Worth extends beyond the client into society through improvements in the economy, including the creation of jobs.

2. **Cost** refers to the total amount of cash paid directly to the client added with any other transaction related expenses such as time, transportation, and taxes. The net gain is calculated by subtracting the costs from the worth.

3. **Depth** refers to how a society values the net gain the client receives from the investment. Different factors such as demographics, geography, and living conditions can all be representative of depth, but loan size is the most usual indicator for depth. Large loan sizes typically increase the benefits society receives but also increase the costs associated with achieving those benefits. Therefore, outreach with high depth can reach those that have the greatest need but requires more financial resources from the investor.

4. **Breadth** simply refers to the volume of investees the MFI partners with. Breadth is heavily dependent on the amount of financial resources the investor can sustain. Therefore, MFIs who follow an institutionalist approach tend to have wider breadth than those that use a welfarist approach.

5. **Length** refers to the duration of time the MFI can continue to offer financing to its clients. A flow of revenue, whether that is from profits or donations, is necessary to achieve length.

6. **Scope** refers to the diversity in the types and terms of financial contracts the MFI offers to its clients. This includes a number of different factors including individualist or group investment preferences and loan repayment policies.

Schreiner asserts that these factors are interrelated and together contribute to an MFI's effectiveness. He also observes that the institutionalist and welfarist approaches (he refers to them as the self-sustainability approach and the poverty approach, respectively) stem from different interpretations of how these factors can and should be applied to microfinance. In order to answer the questions surrounding this topic, Schreiner states that relevant empirical measurements should be the basis for reasoning in any argument supporting the different approaches to microfinance. However, there does not seem to be a universal recognition of the importance of each of the six aspects he describes, and their dependence on one another. Similarly Lebovice, Hermes, and Hudon (2016) observe that existing literature today has come to many different conclusions regarding the underlying trade-off between social and financial goals that differentiates these two approaches.

> ## Distributed Ledger
>
> A database shared with multiple parties that contains a continuously growing chain of transactions between the members of the network.

Distributed Ledger Technology

Traditionally, transactions have been conducted through intermediaries, usually banks, who each maintain their own ledgers (referred to as a centralized ledger). The process is generally conducted as follows: (1) Party A notifies their bank that they wish to transfer funds to Party B, (2) Party A's bank checks their ledger to make sure they have the necessary funds to conduct the transaction, (3) Party A's bank sends the funds to Party B's bank and both banks' ledgers are updated accordingly, (4) Party B's bank notifies him or her that the transfer has been completed. This process is both cost and time inefficient because the communication that occurs between intermediaries can take days, even weeks to complete, and each intermediary requires additional payment. Distributed Ledger Technology (DLT) is a relatively new system for remedying this issue, and many others, with the transaction process.

A distributed ledger (also referred to as a decentralized ledger) is a database shared with multiple parties that contains a continuously growing chain of transactions between the members of the network. Each member, or node, has access to view and update the database as needed through a peer-to-peer network. This system is predicated on a consensus algorithm that sets the guidelines for how each node can access and update the ledger in a reliable and trustworthy manner. However, there is no universal method for achieving this. Each DLT has the ability to develop their own approach to assure only qualified nodes can contribute to the ledger.

A blockchain is the most common way data is stored within a distributed ledger. In a blockchain, the details of each transaction are stored in a "block." This includes a unique identifier for the transaction, a timestamp, a connection to the previous block in the chain, and the transaction data. Once a block is formed, it is linked to the previous block in the chain. The blockchain has a very strict identification system for the blocks that exist within it. In addition, no block in the chain can be removed or altered in any way. If there is a mistake in the ledger, a new transaction must be added to the chain to correct the issue, or the entire chain must be rebuilt. Therefore, a complete log of all conducted transactions, which is incredibly difficult to tamper with, is formed. Implementing this technology dramatically increases transparency in the actions of organizations. This could be revolutionary for social enterprises that struggle with monitoring and reporting systems. Instead of devoting large amounts of resources to developing annual reports and conducting audits, the social enterprise could simply give interested parties access to their network, allowing them to view organizational data at any point. The transparency that this provides not only potentially decreases the financial burden of monitoring and reporting on organizations, but it could also help them to secure funding by increasing trust within their communities.

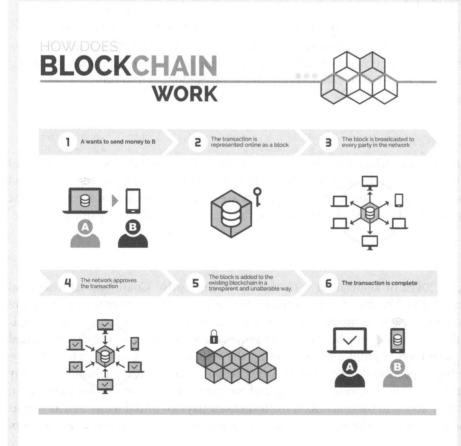

HOW DOES **BLOCKCHAIN** WORK

1 — A wants to send money to B

2 — The transaction is represented online as a block

3 — The block is broadcasted to every party in the network

4 — The network approves the transaction

5 — The block is added to the existing blockchain in a transparent and unalterable way

6 — The transaction is complete

©elenabsl/Shutterstock.com

One of the most significant applications of this technology in the field of social enterprise is the formation of a digital identity. According to the World Bank 2018 data, almost one billion people in the world do not have proof of legal identity. Without access to identification, it can be difficult for individuals to receive a multitude of financial services, work permits, and similar benefits. This is especially true for the multitude of refugees who have recently been disbursed throughout Europe. There are many companies and organizations attempting to capitalize on the potential of blockchain technology for this purpose. One of these is the Finland based personal banking company MONI. MONI is partnering with the Finnish Immigration Service to replace traditional cash disbursements to refugees using blockchain technology. Refugees receive a prepaid MasterCard along with a mobile, customizable payment account. This account also provides them with a digital identity which allows them to receive salary payments and other financial services (https://moni.com/company/the-finnish-immigration-service-chose-monis-smart-payment-service-for-refugees/). However, these effects are not just limited to refugees. According to the World Bank, only 69% of people globally have access to a bank account or a mobile money provider. DLT and digital currency technology could radically change the way charities, social enterprises and other organizations reach these people.

Although this technology shows a lot of promise, it is still in its infancy and many barriers still need to be addressed for it to reach its potential. This includes questions about governmental, social, and legal regulation; network reliability; data storage and retrieval methods; risk management; and more.

Scaling

An entrepreneur who establishes an organization will eventually look to understand how they can scale the organization up, in order to increase both revenue and social impact. While traditional scaling methods are useful, the social entrepreneur must also take into account the ability to scale the social impact of the organization.

Franchise

Temple (2011), in association with the Social Enterprise Coalition, defines social franchising as "the use of a commercial franchising approach to replicate and share proven organizational models for greater social impact." Commercial franchising is a method of growth in which the owner of a company allows an outside individual or organization to build a business using the systems, brand, intellectual property, and other aspects of their company. A representative from the franchising company generally provides ongoing training and support for the new business owner. In return for access to these services, the franchisee pays an initial fee as well as well as ongoing royalties to the franchisor. Temple identifies social franchising as a form of replication that exists on a spectrum (shown below) with different levels of flexibility and control. On one end of the spectrum is dissemination, or open source replication, where all intellectual property surrounding the concept, process, or product is released for anyone to access at no cost. This provides the maximum amount of flexibility for the replicator because the process/product developer has no input into how the replicator uses the technology. On the other end of the spectrum is wholly owned growth where the original organization has exclusive control over the operations of the new entity. Social franchising exists toward the center of this spectrum with slightly more emphasis on input and guidance from the parent organization.

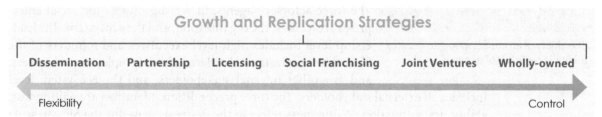

Figure 9.1 Growth and replication strategies

Temple identifies several reasons why an organization, especially a nonprofit, might consider franchising as a method for pursuing social impact. First, it allows the franchisee to focus on impact development without having to go through the process of creating a product, brand, and many other aspects of a new organization that can be difficult to build from scratch. Having access to the knowledge and resources owned by the franchisor regarding these challenges can make start-up much faster and simpler. Also, it allows for flexibility in ownership and decision-making which allows space for entrepreneurial innovation that is aligned with the needs and circumstances surrounding a local population. However, Temple identifies perhaps the most impactful factor of social franchising as the potential to combine social objectives and financial objectives very effectively, but this is only possible if it is implemented correctly and under the right conditions.

Although franchising can be a good opportunity for impact driven organizations, Temple observes that it cannot be recommended in all situations. For example, franchising should not be used as a way to save a struggling business. If the parent company has not fully developed a sustainable financial model, franchising will only duplicate these problems. Temple also notes several issues with franchising that could potentially appear in any social enterprise and need to be carefully monitored by the parties involved. This includes the fact that franchising is often associated with profit-maximization of large corporations. Therefore, effectively conveying the company's story and the purpose of the franchise approach is vital to gather support from investors and the public. Similarly, it is important that the franchisor and franchisee are all united around a common mission and objectives. This can be difficult when the parties involved are potentially focused on double/triple bottom lines outside of financial performance.

Scaling Impact

The ability to scale can be assessed by a framework of understanding the current state and capacity of the leadership, organization, and surrounding ecosystem. In 2016, Thomas Scheuerle & Bjoern Schmitz (2015) released a paper that investigates several of the inhibiting factors social entrepreneurial organizations (SEOs) face in the scaling process. Scheuerle and Schmitz identify the three actors, preconditions, and social forces that outline an SEO's ability to scale effectively by examining data collected from interviews with sixteen SEOs in Germany.

> **Scaling Impact**
>
> The ability of an impact model to grow to meet higher levels of demand.

The three actors, or agents, in **scaling impact** for social enterprises are leaders, the organization, and the ecosystem. The leadership level includes high level executives and founders of the SEO, the organizational level includes all employees, volunteers, and any other internal stakeholders, and the ecosystem level includes all external stakeholders. The three preconditions identified are willingness, ability, and admission. Willingness refers to the desire or drive for the SEO to scale or grow. Ability is the capacity to which the SEO has the skills and resources needed for scaling to be possible. Admission refers to the capability of the SEO to scale without crossing any legal barriers and/or social norms. It is important to note that these preconditions are not absolute and evidence of them is measured over a wide range rather than a dichotomous scale. As a result, progress toward improving these conditions can be achieved during the scaling process, and it is possible, for a short time, that an excess of one condition could compensate for a shortage of another. Lastly, the three social forces identified, originally proposed by Beckert (2010) are cognitive frames, social networks, and institutions. Cognitive frames describe how people behave in different situations due to culturally shared perceptions of reality. One example of this is a funder's preference to invest in newer, more innovative organizations, or more experienced organizations that use tested methods. Social networks are structures which define the relationships between organizations and individuals in a society, such as networks of funders. Lastly, institutions are the laws and cultural values that govern the society.

After conducting the interviews, Scheuerle and Schmitz discovered seventeen inhibiting factors to scaling social impact (shown in the table on the following page).

The framework used in assessing the inhibiting factors takes into account the leaders, organization, and ecosystem of the social enterprise. Each of these has the ability to impact the degree to which an organization is able to scale their social impact.

Inhibiting factor level	Scaling up pre(condition)		
	Willingness Dominant influence of cognitive frames	**Ability** Dominant influence of social networks	**Admission** Dominant influence of institutions
Leaders	• Risk aversion (6) • Percieved threat for social mission (7) • Preference for independence and autonomy (7)	• Lacking business administration skills (3)	
Organization	• Demotivating changes of organizational culture (3)	• Organizational dependency on leaders (9) • Overstraining requirements to staff members (5) • Missing (local) embeddedness (9) • Increasing overhead structures and costs (5) • Difficulties in impact demonstration (6)	• Non-entrepreneurial social legislation and public utility laws (7)
Ecosystem	• Hesitance to provide private capital for scaling up (8) • Reluctance to change and cooperation (10) • Rivalry from entrenched social sector organizations (8)	• Tight financial budgets of local municipalities (4) • Unsuitably qualified workforce (12)	• Inadequate public welfare system funding structures (10)

However, for social enterprises that engage in market-oriented products and services, there is also the assessment that must be made for the growth and scaling of the sale of the goods or services that must be considered. This is due to the dual nature of social enterprises; they must think about the revenue generating aspect of the company and the ability for that aspect to scale, while also thinking about the scalability of the social impact of the organization.

Each of these areas discussed above can also be reviewed to understand how to assess the factors that influence the scalability of the revenue-generating aspect of the company. For example, what are the organizational capacities for growth? What will the investment in the growth cost? And what is the current market share available to grow into for the company.

Fundraising

If the organization is a nonprofit, it has the ability to supplement the revenue provided by the sale of goods and services with the traditional efforts of fundraising. Fundraising can take on a number of different forms, including dinner events, auctions, or soliciting donors for money. In the digital age it is very cost efficient for an organization to send out email blasts to current supporters to solicit funds for various initiatives or projects. However, there is a temptation for fundraising using online means to begin to morph into a method that tries to widen cultural fissures in order to play on the fears and prejudices of individuals, thereby creating an emotional response that is intended to turn into monetary support.

We use the term *cultural arsonists* to describe the organizations that engage in this type of activity, as they work to create "fires" so that they can solicit financial support for their organization. These organizations seek to create anger or fear associated with another group of citizens with the intent to prompt action. The goal is to "keep the enemy at bay" in a cultural sense. Additionally, these efforts can backfire and not only prevent the desired result, but may actually create a more difficult path toward civility. Koenig and McLaughline (2018) state,

> In a perfect world, social causes would encourage a democratic dialogue, but as the literature proposes this is not the norm. Rather, blog posts, comments on Twitter and Facebook, and online petitions are filled with hostility and anxiety. Contextually and theoretically, the snowball of one another's emotions is directly impacting how people relate to social issues. This raises concerns: when those online conversations beget negative emotions, it can be counterproductive or it can be fodder for anxiety. (p. 1673)

This does not mean that organizations should not engage in emotional appeals, but they should do so cautiously, with an eye toward the broader social ramifications of the tone they use to solicit funding.

Conclusion

The ability to raise funds and scale should be understood prior to undertaking a social enterprise, as they are a function of the model and mission of the organization. The effective social entrepreneur looks at the projects at hand, but also has an eye to the future with an understanding of how the organization will scale, both financially and related to the impact that the organization has. While not every social enterprise will have as its focus a large-scale problem, it may be a local issue that is confined to a specific group or geographic location, those who seek to take on large-scale problems should be able to understand what scale would look like and how to effectively work to meet the demand.

References

Anheier, H. K., & Leat, D. (2014, April 30). Philanthropic Foundations: What Rationales? Retrieved April 20, 2018, from https://muse.jhu.edu/article/528215/pdf

Appleyard, L. (2011). Community Development Finance Institutions (CDFIs): Geographies of financial inclusion in the US and UK. Geoforum, *42*(2), 250–258. doi:10.1016/j.geoforum.2010.09.004

Blank, S. (2018, February 09). Why the Lean Start-Up Changes Everything. Retrieved May 2, 2018, from https://hbr.org/2013/05/why-the-lean-start-up-changes-everything

Bos, J. W., & Millone, M. (2012). Practice What You Preach: Microfinance Business Models and Operational Efficiency. SSRN Electronic Journal. doi:10.2139/ssrn.2132456

Bureau of Labor Statistics (2016, April 28). Business establishment age. Retrieved May 2, 2018, from https://www.bls.gov/bdm/entrepreneurship/entrepreneurship.htm

Cassar, G. (2004). The financing of business start-ups. *Journal of Business Venturing*, *19*(2), 261–283. doi:10.1016/s0883-9026(03)00029-6

Corps, M. (2017). Distributed Ledger Technology in Relief & Development. Retrieved from https://www.mercycorps.org/sites/default/files/Mercy-Corps-A-Revolution-in-Trust-Blockchain-May-2017_1.pdf

Koenig, A., & McLaughlin, B. (2018). Change is an emotional state of mind: Behavioral responses to online petitions. *New Media and Society, 20*(4), 1658–1675. https://doi.org/10.1177/1461444817689951

Lebovics, M., Hermes, N., & Hudon, M. (2016). Are Financial and Social Efficiency Mutually Exclusive? A Case Study of Vietnamese Microfinance Institutions. *Annals of Public And Cooperative Economics*, *87*(1), 55–77.

Lahm, R. J., & Little, H. T. (2005). Bootstrapping Business Start-Ups: Entrepreneurship Literature, Textbook, and Teaching Practices Versus Current Business Practices? *Journal of Entrepreneurship Education*, 8, 61–73.

Foundation Center (2014). Foundation Stats: Guide to the Foundation Center's Research Database. Retrieved from http://data.foundationcenter.org/

Foster, W., & Bradach, J. (2005). Should non-profits seek profits. *Harvard Business Review*, (February).

Perry, J. T., Chandler, G. N., Yao, X., & Wolff, J. A. (2011). Bootstrapping Techniques and New Venture Emergence. New England Journal of Entrepreneurship, *14*(1), 35–45. https://doi.org/10.1177/1059601117730574

Porter, M. E., Kramer, M. R. (1999). Philanthropy's New Agenda: Creating Value. Retrieved April 23, 2018, from https://hbr.org/1999/11/philanthropys-new-agenda-creating-value

Scheuerle, T., & Schmitz, B. (2015). Inhibiting factors of scaling up the impact of social entrepreneurial organizations—A comprehensive framework and empirical results for Germany. *Journal of Social Entrepreneurship, 676*(March 2016), 1–35. https://doi.org/10.1080/19420676.2015.1086409

Schreiner, M. (2002). Aspects of outreach: a framework for discussion of the social benefits of microfinance. *Journal of International Development, 14*(5), 591–603. https://doi.org/10.1002/jid.908

Smith, J &, Colgate &, Mark. (2007). Customer Value Creation: A Practical Framework. *Journal of Marketing Theory and Practice, 15*, 7–23. 10.2753/MTP1069-6679150101.

Temple, N. (2011). The Social Franchising Manual (Rep.). London: The Social Enterprise Coalition.

Woller, G. M., Dunford, C., & Woodworth, W. (1999). Where to Microfinance? *International Journal of Economic Development, 1*(1), 29–64. Retrieved April 27, 2018, from http://www.microfinance.com/English/Papers/Where_to_Microfinance.pdf

Ye, Q. (2017). Bootstrapping and new-born startups performance: The role of founding team human capital. *Global Journal of Entrepreneurship, 1*(2), 53–71.

Learning Outcomes

- Distinguish between impact investing and other types of social entrepreneurship
- Summarize different types of impact investments
- Understand barriers to impact investments
- Identify forms of finance related to demand and supply of the impact investment ecosystem

Key Terms

Development Finance Institutions (DFIs)
Global Impact Investing Network (GIIN)
Impact Investing

Program-Related Investments (PRI)
Social Impact Bond (SIB)

Introduction

Impact investing is a recent term that has arisen as a way to describe investments that have a positive social and financial return (Höchstädter, A. K., & Scheck, B, 2015). This type of investing is beyond the individual support of donations from individuals or corporations to nonprofits or charities, but repre-

Impact Investing

Investments into companies where social return is a value for the investor.

sents a way to bring together those who are willing to be investors in companies that have a blended value proposition and can serve to realize a return for the investors beyond financial value. As we begin to dive deeper into the concept and application of impact investing, we will first discuss the definition of impact investing. Impact investing is not the same as a social finance, which can include the broader financing of social enterprises such as grants or donations.

Growth of Socially Responsible Investing

The term *impact investing* was coined by the Rockefeller Foundation in 2007 (Innovative Finance), but the combination of financial objectives and social impact objectives was not a new concept at that time. Organizations such as Acumen Fund, who began investing patient capital in businesses located in Asia and Africa, had explored the concept years before the Rockefeller Foundation created the term. However, the Rockefeller Foundation was the first to attempt a widespread push toward collaboration between actors within the industry. They believed this was needed to develop the industry into a worldwide force for investing in social/environmental impact (Harji & Jackson, 2012).

Although the impact investing industry has seen much growth over the past decade, there has yet to be a universally agreed upon definition for the term. One of the major actors in the industry, the Global Impact Investing Network (GIIN), defines impact investments as, "investments made into companies, organizations, and funds with the intention to generate social and environmental impact alongside a financial return" (What is Impact Investing, 2018). This definition is very broad which makes it difficult to identify what exactly constitutes an impact investment. However, Trelstad (2016) believes that this was, to some extent, intentional because of the GIIN's desire to highlight the potential scale of the industry. Trelstad also observed that the current definition presents another, more significant issue with impact investing. This issue is whether impact investments can realistically provide the investor with a financial return that compares to a profit maximizing investment, while also providing a social return greater than if the investor had given a philanthropic donation using the excess funds made from a profit maximizing investment. Trelstad believes the only way to answer this is by continuing to gather data to evaluate the performance of impact investments in the market. This may sound simple, but it is not an easy task.

Another factor that has had a large impact on the industry is the need for impact measurement tools. The first push to develop a universal language and reporting standards for the impact investing industry came in the form of the Impact Reporting and Investment Standards (IRIS). The IRIS was formed in 2008 by a collaboration between the Rockefeller Foundation and the Acumen Fund, and has been helpful to social entrepreneurs by increasing the transparency and credibility of their organizations operations and impact measurement data (https://iris.thegiin.org/about-iris). After the development of the IRIS, the Global Impact Investing Ratings System (GIIRS) was formed to provide a structure for rating investments, mostly for organizations that utilize debt and equity financing rather than venture philanthropy. The IRIS, GIIRS, and other impact measuring methodologies have been important in the development of the impact investing industry. However, there is still much to be learned about these investments, and new or improved tool need to be developed to assist investment professionals in this pursuit (Trelstad, 2016).

Defining Impact Investing

Efforts to invest with an impact have existed for decades, but the term was officially coined in 2007. With recent worldwide trends showing an increase in initiatives such as corporate social responsibility and impact investing, it is important to have a uniform definition of the term. With scholars using the term *impact investing* interchangeably with others, an official definition is needed to show consistency in the literature. One study that aimed at narrowing down and defining what exactly is meant by impact investing contributed to the current literature in three ways.

Hochstadter & Scheck (2015) found there was much agreement in the literature and between scholars when it came to the two crucial elements of impact investing: non-financial and financial returns. The research showed that some current criteria for nonfinancial returns must be measurable, but it should be noted that there was not a commonality within the literature to show that some impact investors place more emphasis on getting a nonfinancial return over their financial return, while others place more of an emphasis on financial returns over nonfinancial returns.

Additionally, Hochstadter & Scheck (2015), clarified how similar terms in the literature relate to impact investing. For example, the study showed how the term social investment is used synonymously with the term impact investing. Research has also shed light on the fact that there have been recent efforts to bring the terms *impact investing* and *social investment* together with the new term *social impact investing*. Research has shown that the term *socially responsible investing* is distinctly different from impact investing but does not seem to indicate why that is.

Finally, the study showed the strategic options that exist around impact investing. Research has shown that impact investing is a diverse option in regards to who can be impacted, where they can be impacted and how to finance these impacts. For example, impact investing can take place in developing countries or even developed countries and reach a number of sectors from education to healthcare and is not limited to a specific asset class.

Models of Impact Investing

Social Impact Bond (SIB)

A Social Impact Bond (SIB) is a contract between government agencies and private investors where the investors agree to fund public initiatives that achieve a social outcome (Giacomantonio, 2017). These outcomes ideally result in savings for the public sector which are, in part, returned to the investor. In theory, SIB seems to be an attractive form of impact investment for both the commissioner and the investor. However, there are several issues that have caused them to take up a relatively small portion of the total impact investing market.

> **Social Impact Bond (SIB)**
>
> A contract between government agencies and private investors where the investors agree to fund public initiatives that achieve a social outcome.

One of these issues is that SIB is still fairly new (first implemented in 2010). Since there is little data on their effectiveness, many investors have found it difficult to forecast returns and, as a result, find these investments riskier. Similarly, the lack of standardization in contracting of these investments has caused many disagreements between investors and commissioners which has incentivized investors to pursue other forms of investment. Not only do these contracting disputes introduce an element of uncertainty into these negotiations, but they also result in very high fixed transaction costs. Also, completion of these contracts often requires evaluation of the initiatives used to create impact. This further adds costs to these contracts that are not typically associated with other kinds of impact investing.

Possibly the most influential factor responsible for the lack of adoption of SIBs in the investment market is the paradox that occurs between investors and commissioners. From the commissioner's point of view, although it may result in a positive financial return utilizing an SIB, a successful initiative will, in most cases, yield a greater financial return if they use another source of funding. On the other hand, a failed initiative results in a complete loss of the investors' investment (successful initiatives, if they do not result in the savings predicted, could also result in partial loss of investment). Therefore, if maximizing financial return is the primary goal of both parties, using an SIB is rarely the best option. However, this could be seen as an attractive option for commissioners who want to minimize the risk of their investment because almost all losses are incurred by the investor in this situation. Therefore, SIBs are best used as a financial investment strategy when the likelihood of a successful initiative cannot be determined by one or both parties, or when the commissioner wants to divert risk away from themselves.

SIB may be successful as a form of philanthropic venture capital for grant-funding agencies who operate under a limited budget. By spreading out their grant funding across multiple SIB, they have the ability to fund multiple projects while retaining at least a portion of the funds they give out. As mentioned before, SIBs have significantly higher transaction costs than other forms of funding, but most other funding options are guaranteed to result in a complete loss of funds for the investor. Therefore, an SIB could be a viable option in the investor believer the financial savings from utilizing an SIB outweigh the added transaction costs.

Patient Capital

Harrison, Botelho, and Mason (2016) define patient capital as, "capital held by owners who have long time horizons, allowing them to endure the uncertain early years of an investment and reap high returns in the longer term." Although these investments do not specifically need to be backed by a desire to solve a social issue, the term is often associated with social ventures (Harrison, 2016). Patient capital is especially useful for entrepreneurs in developing nations due to a lack of infrastructure, high levels of corruption, and very low personal incomes. Entrepreneurs in these conditions have a very hard time securing traditional forms of investment capital. Although these investments are more focused on helping the entrepreneur succeed, they do require a financial return that shows the business can achieve long-term sustainability (https://acumen.org/about/patient-capital/).

Development Finance Institutions

<table>
<tr><td>

Development Finance Institutions (DFIs)

Specialized development banks that are dedicated to strengthening the private sector in developing nations.

</td><td>

Development Finance Institutions (DFIs) are specialized development banks that are dedicated to strengthening the private sector in developing nations. National governments are generally the entities that own a majority share in these institutions. DFIs can be backed by a singular government that seeks to

</td></tr>
</table>

implement its own development and cooperation policies (bilateral), or by multiple governments that work together (multilateral). However, not every DFI is structured the same. Some are owned completely by government, but some also allow partial ownership by private investors.

Program Related Investments

A **program-related investment (PRI)** is "a loan, equity investment, or guaranty, made by a foundation in pursuit of its charitable mission rather than to generate income" (Brest, 2016) These investments can be made to both nonprofits and for-profits, but for-profits are the primary recipients. For an investment to be considered a PRI, it must be aligned with at least one of the investing foundation's exempt purposes and must not be utilized for impacting political elections and legislation or property appreciation/income production. PRIs come with an expectation that the investor will not receive market-rate returns or potentially incur in a loss.

Therefore, they should not be treated as an investment in the investor's portfolio. On the other hand, they should not be treated as a grant because they result in at least part of the principal being repaid. However, a PRI gives the investing foundation access to certain rights that do not normally accompany a grant. This includes the right to appoint board members and a priority claim on assets if the organization fails to focus on their charitable contribution or goes bankrupt.

Street Food Institute

Street Food Institute (SFI) is a 501(c)3 nonprofit organization based in Albuquerque, New Mexico. SFI was started in 2014 as a partnership with Central New Mexico Community College (CNM) where they offered training to culinary students on how to operate food trucks and similar forms of mobile food businesses. Today, they have extended these services to the community in the form of a twelve-week training program for young aspiring entrepreneurs who want to learn how to start and main-

©ESB Professional/Shutterstock.com

tain a successful small food business. They hope that inspiring and empowering entrepreneurship will help rebuild New Mexico's struggling economy through job creation and the development of local business opportunities. SFI has three main sources of funding: revenue from their food trucks, catering business, and their café (operated on campus at Central New Mexico Community College); grants and donations; and tuition from their entrepreneurial classes. However, they are dedicated to finding new and improved ways to increase their revenues so that they can decrease their dependence on donations and grants.

The state of New Mexico is currently experiencing high rates of poverty and low rates of education completion. These conditions have created a high need for economic support in many communities. However, very few foundations and individuals have shown interest in investing in the state. This has resulted in a large number of nonprofit organizations competing for a very limited amount of available funding. Since a portion of SFI's revenue is generated by grants and donations, competition with other organizations is a constant challenge. This also highlights the need for more sustainable approaches to solving the many needs of their communities.

Effectiveness of Impact Investing

In the beginning of 2013, the social investment market in the UK was assessed to determine its impact on the economy (ICF, GHK, 2013). For some time, the investment activity has been increasing in the UK, but there has not been data to show this trend. This research was conducted to show the impact on the economy that social investment is having at a national and regional level. This was measured through the lending activity of Social Investment Finance Intermediaries (SIFI) when it came to jobs in the UK, businesses, turnover, and value added. This data was collected by sending a survey to all Social Investment Finance Intermediaries in the UK as well as sending a survey to the social ventures in the UK that have received social investment funding.

Additionally, the research was also conducted because social enterprises are creating jobs for approximately two million people in the UK and significantly contributing to the economy but their impact is limited to some extent due to financing opportunities. It is estimated that there is a large funding gap for these ventures.

The research found that the social investment market grew by almost a quarter from 2010 to 2012. There were twenty-nine social investment financing intermediaries that were led by four social banks. The study also found that there was a high concentration on the investments toward three primary organizations. It was interesting to note that the study did find that there was a great diversity in the coverage. There was not one sector, region or social outcome that received more attention than others.

This research has great implications for the UK as a whole. For example, the research shows the great value the social investment market has in society, not just from a social aspect but also from an economic aspect. Research showing that there was social investment market growth rate of a quarter from 2010 to 2012 while Social Investment Financing Intermediaries only met half of the need of social ventures, proves that there is still a large gap in place. Without resources to meet this gap there will be a continued lack of social benefits and even reduced growth in the UK's economy (ICF/GHK, 2013). Research indicates this gap can be partially filled by smaller SIFIs, which will be help reach more social ventures.

Barriers to Growth of Impact Investing

A study from the World Economic Forum looked at assessing the impact investment sector and identifying what factors are constraining capital into this sector. The study looked at five areas: motivation and focus of the initiative, defining impact investing, what the sector currently looks like, the constraints potential investors face, and recommendations for the future.

Looking at motivation and scope, it has been concluded that the main asset owners making impact investments are development finance entities, family offices, and individuals who are of high-net-worth. It should be noted that the study also concluded that, for the sector to realize its full potential, the other types of owners will be required to make impact investments. Next, the study defines and provides examples of what exactly impact investing is and how it differs from traditional investing. The study cites examples of asset owners making investments to generate social and/or environmental gains while also generating financial gains. The research study also points out that the state of the impact investing sector is growing. While in the past most of the investments have been driven by niche entities, there has been a recent expansion to include mainstream investors. Next, the study was able to identify several major constraints that asset owners are confronted with when trying to make impact investments so that an action plan can be created to address these constraints. The study identified the constraints in four areas: early-stage ecosystem, small average deal size, fit within asset allocation framework, and double bottom line. Finally, this study looked at what exactly can be done moving forward to advance impact investing toward the mainstream investors. The study concluded that many entities will need to work together to make this happen. For example, impact investment funds will have to work with impact enterprises and foundations and even the government.

Glanzel and Scheuerle (2015) assessed the major factors that inhibit impact investment in Germany. Their study was comprised of interviews with nineteen different actors in the impact investing process, including investing funds, investment advisors, and social entrepreneurs. However, the concept of impact investing covers a wide range of expected returns. On one end of the spectrum, there are impact-first investors who require little or no financial return from their investment. On the other end, finance-first impact investors place less emphasis on the social returns of their investment and are primarily focused on the financial returns (Hebb, 2013). This study is centered around impact-first investors and adopts the term "social impact investing" to better represent its point of view. Glanzel and Scheuerle observed eight different areas of concern all relating to the dimensions of social returns, financial returns, or relationships between the actors and the surrounding infrastructure.

The first dimension Glanzel and Scheuerle observed was the feasibility of achieving financial return on investment when the organization focuses on a social issue. The first factor they observed within this dimension was insecure income models. The structure of Germany's social welfare quasimarkets can often have a large effect on a social enterprise's ability to obtain social impact investments. These inflexible funding structures often hurt innovative social enterprises by causing their income to be based more on outside forces, such as political changes, rather than the organization's performance or target group demand. Also, due to recent uncovering of misuse of funding in several large nonprofit organizations, many private donors have started to require all their funds to go directly to the social enterprise's target group. This prevents social enterprises from building capacity, management, marketing, and other forms of overhead that are necessary for scaling impact, and as a result, hurts their chances for securing social impact investments. Another financial issue arises when the target group's lack of resources prevents the social enterprise from obtaining enough revenue to pay back investors. Even though there is likely a large potential for social impact in these areas, it is unlikely that achieving this impact will directly provide the organization with financial returns. This often makes creating sustainable business models difficult. Another factor that impedes social impact investment is the lack of business skills in many social entrepreneurs. Without the ability to create and carry out proper business plans, social entrepreneurs can find it challenging to attract investors. Lastly, differing perceptions of risk were found to impede social impact investments. Some investors view the innovative nature of social enterprises as high risk due to the small amount of experience both the social entrepreneur and investor usually have in the work being done. However, some investors see investing in social enterprises as equal or lower risk than convental venture capital because of the general perception of social entrepreneurs as ethically and morally grounded individuals.

Within the social return dimension, Glanzel and Scheuerle observed several inhibiting factors. First of all, they observed that many social enterprises believe that the social value they create is largely undervalued in investment contracts. This is believed to occur because of the lack of a consistent method for quantifying social returns. This makes investment decisions difficult for investors because of their obligations to capital providers. Also, social impact investors often require extensive reporting on social returns. This, coupled with a lack of standardized tools for measuring outcomes and linking them to the activities of the social enterprise, has made it difficult for social enterprises to prove their legitimacy and secure social impact investments.

Within the relationships and infrastructure dimension, Glanzel and Scheuerle observed that there are often barriers between social enterprises and social impact investors in the form of language, attitudes, and convictions. For example, one interviewee found that often, "It's not institutions negotiating with institutions, but people with people." She went on to describe the fact that analyzing how individual investors will react to people of different professional backgrounds, demographics, and other personal traits can have a profound impact on the likelihood of receiving an investment. They also found that social enterprises value autonomy very highly. However, investors often place restrictions on social enterprises and push for access to decision-making power because of their desire to mitigate risk. Although the view that investors can bring to the table certain skills and knowledge not possessed by the social enterprise is often valid, many social enterprises believe this restricts their ability take the risks necessary for their start-up to be successful. They also believe that many of these factors that impede social impact investments could be solved by different intermediary organizations. These intermediaries could assist in developing agreements between the parties based on decision-making structures, knowledge and tool development, and transparency within the organizations.

Article Summaries

In the UK, each year there are approximately 42,000 adults released back into the streets after serving less than one year in prison. With the prison system costing taxpayers in the UK over £213 million per year, there are few initiatives to help these former prisoners stay out of prison in the future, which result in approximately 73% going back to prison.

There seems to be a trend in the UK when it comes to government spending on preventative spending versus intervention spending. Research shows that the UK government spends more on intervening once a problem has already occurred rather than focus its spending on ways to prevent that problem in the first place.

In the past trusts and foundations have taken an initiative to limit the number of individuals needing intervention. But with limited resources these charitable trusts and foundations can only do so much to make an impact. As a result of this limitation there has emerged a new financing option: Social Impact Bonds. Social Impact Bonds are an initiative to raise nongovernment investments that invest in early intervention and prevention initiatives to reach the root cause of issues those individuals in society deal with. This takes a different approach from traditional spending, in which a lot of money is wasted on crisis intervention. With Social Impact Bonds placing emphasis on early root cause interventions, there are better social outcomes and less need for crisis intervention resources. The basis of these bonds are for the government to use a percentage of the money that they are saving as a result of these bonds initiatives working and reward the nongovernment investors.

Von Schnurbein, Georg; Fritz, Tizian; Mani, S. (2015). Social impact bonds, 13(August), 1–8.

Case Study Example

The New Market Tax Credit gives investors the opportunity to reduce the amount they would owe the government through taxes by investing in a qualified community development entity. These entities take the funds received by investors and allocate them to low-income community initiatives such as real estate development or funding businesses.

In order to allow low income communities to start experiencing the economic boom that the rest of the nation was experiencing in the early 2000s many legislators sought to pass legislation that would allow individuals to invest in these communities and experience a tax relief as the result of their investment. This was one way to get a flow of capital into these regions since they were not going to be able to come up with it on their own.

The Community Development Entity is the intermediary between the investor and the low income community. To qualify as a CDE, an entity's main mission must be to serve low income communities and also must be held accountable by a community board participation.

Thomley, B., Wood, D., Grace, K., & Sarah, S. (2011). Impact investing: A framework for policy design and analysis. *Pacific Community*, 104. Retrieved from http://www.rockefellerfoundation.org/uploads/files/88fdd93f-b778-461e-828c-5c5 26ffed184-impact.pdf

Implementing Social Impact Investing

In 2014, the Social Impact Investment Taskforce (SIIT) released a report that identifies several recommendations for governments to implement social impact more effectively and efficiently. However, the SIIT recognizes that each country has different governmental and economic structures that affect its impact investing ecosystem. The report defines an impact investing ecosystem as a combination of impact seeking purchasers, impact-driven organizations, forms of finance, channels of impact capital, and sources of impact capital. Because these structures are different in every country, the report attempts to make recommendations that can be implemented universally under many different conditions. Recommendations for specific individual countries can be found in the reports created by separate national advisory boards.

The SIIT recommendations focus around a few different categories. The first category is reducing the limits placed on impact seeking organizations. This includes opening opportunities for entrepreneurs to obtain capital when in the early stages of development, creating access to markets, and creating policies that incentivize impact investment. They also place emphasis on impact measurement. Impact measurement is necessary for multiple pieces in the impact investment process including governments, foundations, social sector organizations, impact driven businesses, and impact investors. Improving the way organizations analyze and report the social value they add would allow them to achieve greater outcomes and make these investments more attractive to the other parties involved. They also believe impact investment may have a much larger impact on developing countries than developed. However, this will require cooperation between many important actors including governments, investors, international institutions, foundations, and individual citizens.

The Impact Investor

There has been very little information regarding the performance of impact investing, and the information that exists is dispersed between different regions and sectors. In 2011, J.P Morgan, alongside the Global Impact Investing Network, conducted a two-part survey intended to observe the characteristics that define these investors, and develop a broad understanding of the market that connects these regions and sectors (Saltuk, Y., Bouri, A., & Leung, G., 2011).

Seventy-five percent of the fifty-two survey respondents labeled the impact investing market as a market still in its infancy but growing. They noted that the number of investors who are familiar with impact investing doubled between 2010 and 2011 and continues to grow. However, there are several factors that are hindering growth in the industry. These factors include a lack of track record for successful investments, a shortage of quality investment opportunities, and inadequate impact measurement practices. Despite these issues, and more, investors generally seem to be cautiously optimistic about the future of the industry. This is due, in part, to increased support from government and improvements to infrastructure. These infrastructure improvements have helped to increase transparency within social impact organizations and help investors gage their performance to make better investing decisions. A few examples of this are the Impact Reporting and Investment Standards (IRIS), ImpactBase, and ImpactAssets.

The next topic the researchers explored was the relationship between impact and financial returns. One common view of this interaction is that to increase financial returns from an investment, a portion of the impact must be sacrificed, and vice versa. However, others believe that one is not dependent on the other and both can be maximized without compromise. When the survey participants were asked about this topic, 62% stated that they would sacrifice financial returns in order to achieve greater impact. Similarly, 60% of the respondents believed that making this trade-off was not necessary when making investments. These results are shown in the figures below.

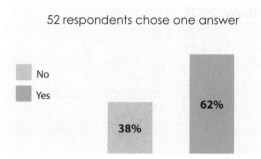

Figure 10.1 As an impact investor, would you sacrifice financial returns for greater impact?

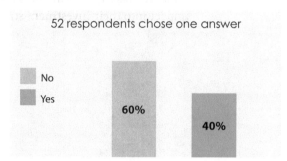

Figure 10.2 Generally speaking, do you think a trade-off between financial returns and impact is necessary wen making impact investments?

Adapted from GIIN, J.P. Morgan.

Also, only 46% of the respondents stated that they balance both financial returns and impact when making investments while the other 54% prefer to optimize one over the other (shown in Figure 10.3 below). Although this data was taken from a relatively small sample of all investors, it does point to the conclusion that investors take a wide range of approaches when considering investments. They also observed that 58% of the respondents focused on social impact as their primary impact objective, as opposed to only 8% that prioritized environmental (shown in Figure 10.4 below). Another interesting fact is that 94% of reported investments were directed toward helping low-income groups.

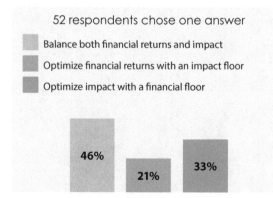

Figure 10.3 Investment thesis

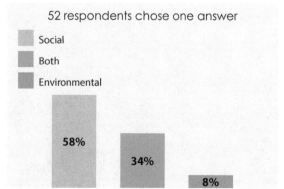

Figure 10.4 Primary impact objective

Adapted from GIIN, J.P. Morgan.

Conclusion

Impact investing's goal of generating financial returns as well as social or environmental returns is gaining more popularity in this day in age. While it may be simple to track a financial return, it is not always as simple to track a social or environmental return. But with investors wanting to see just exactly the impact their investment is making in the world, measuring this impact is becoming more needed. For example, many investors look to measurement data to communicate their impact for the sake of marketing or even fundraising. While there have been strides in reporting through various projects and organizations such as the Impact Management Fund and the Global Impact Investing Network, there still remains a gap in the effectiveness of measuring impact. In the future, investors will likely not look toward measuring as a way to meet requirements for reporting purposes, but as a way to integrate their impact into their investment strategy (Schultz, 2017).

References

Giacomantonio, C. (2017). Grant-Maximizing but not Money-Making: A Simple Decision-Tree Analysis for Social Impact Bonds. *Journal of Social Entrepreneurship, 8*(1), 1–20. https://doi.org/10.1080/19420676.2016.1271348

Glänzel, G., & Scheuerle, T. (2016). Social Impact Investing in Germany: Current Impediments from Investors' and Social Entrepreneurs' Perspectives. *Voluntas*. https://doi.org/10.1007/s11266-015-9621-z

Harji, K., & Jackson, E. T. (2012). Accelerating Impact: Achievements, Challenges and What's next in building the Impact Investing Industry. The Rockefeller Foundation, (July), 86.

Harrison, R. T., Botelho, T., & Mason, C. M. (2016). Patient Capital in Entrepreneurial Finance: A Reassessment of the Role of Business Angel Investors. Socio-Economic Review, *14*(4), 66–689.

Höchstädter, A. K., & Scheck, B. (2015). What's in a Name: An Analysis of Impact Investing Understandings by Academics and Practitioners. *Journal of Business Ethics, 132*(2), 449–475. https://doi.org/10.1007/s10551-014-2327-0

Innovative Finance (https://www.rockefellerfoundation.org/our-work/initiatives/innovative-finance/)

ICF GHK. (2013). Growing the social investment market: the landscape and economic impact, (July), 1–72.

Saltuk, Y., Bouri, A., & Leung, G. (2011). Insight into the impact investment market. *Building Standards*, (December), 5–7.

Schultz, A. (2017, December 19). Impact Investors Make Strides in Measuring Results. Retrieved February 02, 2018, from https://www.barrons.com/articles/impact-investors-make-strides-in-measuring-results-1513703972

Social Impact Investment Taskforce (2014). Impact investment: The invisible heart of markets, (September), 30. Retrieved from https://impactinvestingaustralia.com/wp-content/uploads/Social-Impact-Investment-Taskforce-Report-FINAL.pdf

Thomley, B., Wood, D., Grace, K., & Sarah, S. (2011). Impact investing: A framework for policy design and analysis. *Pacific Community*, 104. Retrieved from http://www.rockefellerfoundation.org/uploads/files/88fdd93f-b778-461e-828c-5c526ffed184-impact.pdf

Trelstad, B. (2016). Impact Investing: A brief history. Capitalism and Society, *11*(2), 1–14.

Von Schnurbein, Georg; Fritz, Tizian; Mani, S. (2015). Social impact bonds, *13*(August), 1–8.

World Economic Forum (2013). From the margins to the mainstream assessment of the impact investment sector and opportunities to engage mainstream investors, (September), 40. Retrieved from http://www3.weforum.org/docs/WEF_II_FromMarginsMainstream_Report_2013.pdf

GIIN (2018). What is Impact Investing? https://thegiin.org/impact-investing/need-to-know/#what-is-impact-investing

Glossary

Agent Theory: A theory that posits that individuals do break out of socially established structures and seek the change of those structures through creativity and action.

Alignment: A consistent agreement between the social mission and the market orientation of a social enterprise.

Audience: The potential customers and supporters of a company, brand, or product, toward whom the brand story is aimed or crafted.

Backstory: The history of a company or creator, offering the reason for product creation or a company coming into existence; the "why" behind the current company or product.

BACO (Best Available Charitable Option) Ratio: A way to compare the impact of direct investment of funds and donations to charitable organizations to solve social issues.

Balance Sheet: A financial statement that provides a picture of the firm's assets and liabilities at a certain moment in time, used to monitor and analyze the firm's financial position.

Balanced Scorecard: A document that lays out the big picture goals of the organization and the initiatives the organization will use to achieve those goals.

Benefit Corporation (B Corp): A for-profit company that has demonstrated a dual mission to making profits and promoting social good.

Bootstrapping: A variety of nontraditional techniques used by entrepreneurs to generate startup funding and/or reduce the costs associated with starting a business.

Brand: The name, term, sign, symbol, or design, or any combination of the previous, intended to identify the goods and services of one seller or group of sellers and to differentiate them from those of other sellers.

Business Model: The plan the business has to convert resources to meet market demand for a product or service while taking into account costs and revenue.

Calling: The compulsion that an individual feels in pursuing a particular activity.

Character: The main people in a story—here the brand or the customer—that have the greatest effect on the plot or are the most affected by the events of the story; they are relatable, take action, and have articulated goals.

Community Contribution Corporation (CCC): A business distinction that exists in Canada as an attempt by the Canadian government to develop a social enterprise distinction that is able to exist to meet the needs of the social entrepreneurs in the country.

Community Foundation: A publicly supported charity that exists as a vehicle for communities to set up trusts that are directed toward activities, specifically related to improving the community in which it operates.

Community Interest Corporation (CIC): A legal status that is available to companies in the United Kingdom through the Office of the Regulator of Community Interest Companies.

Consumer Values: The principles or items that consumers regard as important.

Conventional Entrepreneurship: The efforts of an individual or group to establish a successful business venture from concept to implementation.

Cooperatives: An enterprise that is owned and operated by the members of that organization.

Corporate Social Responsibility: The activities in which an organization shows that they recognize the social impact of their business.

Credit: The ability to have access to goods or services on the condition of future payment.

Culture: The collective social values and systems in which a market operates.

Demand: A desire or need for a service or product.

Development Finance Institutions (DFIs): Specialized development banks that are dedicated to strengthening the private sector in developing nations.

Differentiated Hybrid: Whenever the consumers or audience of the commercial activities are separate from the audience that is the recipient of the social benefit and value.

Distributed Ledger: A database shared with multiple parties that contains a continuously growing chain of transactions between the members of the network.

Economic Conditions: The financial state of a country or region.

Effective Altruism: Activity engaged in for the good of others in a systematic and measurable way.

Engagement: The process of forming an emotional or rational attachment between a consumer and a brand; it is most well recognized in marketing terms as brand engagement or customer engagement.

Expected Return: An estimate found by multiplying the outcome, likelihood of success, and the philanthropic contribution, then dividing by the cost.

For-Profit: A tax distinction and governance model that allows an organization to distribute profits to shareholders.

Fundraising: The organized activity for raising funds. It can take on a number of different forms, including dinner events, auctions, or soliciting donors for money.

Global Impact Investing Network (GIIN): A global network of impact investors who share resources and information related to impact investing.

Impact Investing: Investments into companies where social return is a value for the investor.

Innovation: The dimension of social entrepreneurship concerned with seeking new or more effective ways to solve problems.

Integrated Hybrid: A type of organization in which the beneficiaries of social value and the customers or consumers of the product or service are the same individuals.

Intrapreneurship: The process of creatively seeking to use new methods or models to solve problems within an organization.

Inverse Demand: The condition in which a social enterprise seeks to reduce the demand for the social impact while increasing the demand for the sale of their products or services.

Lean Start-up: A start-up that trades traditional straight-line product development for a more agile approach with a focus on customer development.

Low-Profit Limited Liability Company (L3C): A business distinction allowed by the government whereby a company can add in different ownership structures to the members, with varying levels of decision making.

Market Orientation: The aspect of social entrepreneurship that seeks to supply goods and services in response to consumer demand.

Market: An area that facilitates the exchange of goods or services between individuals or groups.

Microfinance: The provision of small loans to businesses or individuals for the purpose of alleviating poverty.

Mission Drift: The risk social enterprises face of diverting more and more attention away from their social mission due to increased pressure to generate revenue.

Model of Change: A description the factors that are a part of transformation processes.

Motivation: The driving force behind why an individual engages in certain behavior.

Nonprofit: A tax distinction and governance model that requires an organization to reinvest profits back into the organization.

Opportunity Recognition: The identification of a use for a method or model to solve an existing problem.

Organizational Behavior: The interactions that takes place between members in an organization.

Organizational Culture: The formal and informal values that drive the behavior of individuals in an organization.

Personnel: The individuals who are a formal part of an organization and contribute to the goals of the business.

Political System: The method of governance in place in a particular population that enacts and enforces laws.

Private Ownership: Ownership of property or assets by an individual or group of individuals, as opposed to a government or public entity. Process: A series of actions or steps taken in order to achieve a particular end. In the storytelling and branding process, process is a systematic approach used to create, communicate, and strengthen a firm's brand. It consists of a number of sequential steps. These steps may vary depending on who is implementing the process and the specific outcomes the firm is trying to achieve.

Profit and Loss (P&L) Statement: A financial statement that shows how profitable the firm is over the course of a year.

Program-Related Investment (PRI): Investment made by a foundation with the intent of furthering a mission, as opposed to generating income.

Return on Equity: A measure of how much profit is made per dollar of investment from shareholders.

Revenue: The inflow of financial returns to a company.

Scaling Impact: The ability of an impact model to grow to meet higher levels of demand.

Social Change Theories: Proposed explanations regarding the forces that precipitate changes in society.

Social Entrepreneurship: The process of leveraging market demand for goods and services to provide a sustainable, positive change in society.

Social Impact Bond (SIB): A contract between government agencies and private investors where the investors agree to fund public initiatives that achieve a social outcome.

Social Performance Measurement: The method by which a social enterprise measures the effect of their activities on the desired social change.

Social Values: Those principles that a society deems as important and worthy of high regard.

Sociality: The aspect of social entrepreneurship that is concerned with the measurable social impact.

Stakeholders: Those members of a society who are affected by business activity.

Storytelling: The act of explaining the concepts, beliefs, and values of a company or brand through stories, inviting the audience to recognize identifiable characters and empathize with their experiences. Stories acknowledge beliefs that are already in place, amplifying them with emotion and connection.

Structuration Theory: A belief or policy that places limits on the individual and confines the activity of the agent to the social forces in which the individual operates.

Value Proposition: The physical and nonphysical items that are provided to another in a market-based exchange that an individual deems to be important.

Value-Added Transactions: The measurable benefit to individuals who engage in a market transaction.

Values: The principles or items that an individual holds as important.

Virtual Teams: A group of individuals who work together in an organization but do not meet or communicate in the same physical location.

Voluntary Exchange: An event in which an individual or group has the freedom to make exchanges of goods or services in accordance with their wants or needs.

Volunteers: Individuals who work toward the mission of an organization but do not receive payment for their services.

Index

entrepreneurial activity, 35
entrepreneur, profile of
    behavior, 23–24
    motivation and values, 24
equity financing, 138
equity investment, 141
expected return (ER), 87–88
experimentation, idea of, 101

F

Feeding America, 33
financial crisis (2008), 10
financial exclusion, problem of, 127
financial systems, 34
    foundations, 125–126
    lenders, 126–134
    start-up financing, 123–125
Fisher, Walter, 110
for-profit institutions, 7, 57, 58, 62, 66, 69, 102–103
foundations, charitable, 125–126
    origins of, 125
    public perception of, 126
free-market system, 6, 31
    capitalism, 9
    economies, 31
    of exchanges, 33
Friedman, Milton, 9
funding
    fundraising activities, 63
    short and long term, 71
fundraising, 63, 123, 134

G

Ganley, Barbara, 116
Global Impact Investing Network (GIIN), 90, 138, 146, 148
Global Impact Investing Ratings System (GIIRS), 138
Global Reporting Initiative, 65
Global Slavery Index, 68
goal-setting stories, 117
Goodwill Industries International, Inc., 64

governance, of company, 72
Grameen Bank, 4, 35
Grayson, P. D., 101

H

High Impact Giving Guide, 87
hiring, in social enterprises, 95
hybrid organization
    differentiated, 56
    integrated, 56

I

ImpactAssets, 147
ImpactBase, 147
impact investing
    article summaries, 144–145
    barriers to growth of, 142–144
    case study, 145
    definition of, 137, 138–139
    effectiveness of, 142–144
    elements of, 138
    financial returns, 138
    goal of generating financial returns, 148
    models of
        Development Finance Institutions (DFIs), 140
        patient capital, 140
        program-related investment (PRI), 141
        Social Impact Bond (SIB), 139–140
    nonfinancial, 138
    performance of, 146
    socially responsible investing and, 137–138
impact investors, 146–147
Impact Management Fund, 148
Impact Reporting and Investment Standards (IRIS), 90, 138, 147
information collection, 49
information gathering, 49
infrastructure system, 39
innovation, concept of, 20, 22, 48, 52
integrated hybrids, 56

operating profit margin, 81
opportunity recognition, concept of, 40,
  45, 47
organizational behavior
  conflict resolution, 100–101
  defined, 94
  entrepreneurial, 94
  hiring, 95
  intrapreneurship, 101
  mission drift, 103–104
  personnel, 94
  teams, 96–97
  virtual teams, 98–99
  volunteers, 96
organizational capacity, 82
organizational culture, 101
  creation of, 104–105
  primary drivers of, 105
organizational ownership. *See*
 ownership of company
organizational stakeholders, 96
organizational structure, of social
 enterprise
  benefit corporation, 65
  business model of, 53–57, 61
  community contribution corporation
   (CCC), 66
  Community Foundation, 64–65
  community interest company (CIC),
   66–68
  considerations, 71
  cooperatives, 69–70
  funding aspect of, 71
  fundraising activities, 63
  governance, 72
  low-profit limited liability
   company, 69
  mission drift and accountability, 70
  nonprofit companies, 64
  ownership, 71
  personal liability, 71
  private ownership, 63
  profit distribution, 72
  traditional structures, limitations of,
   62–63
Osterwalder, A., 55

ownership of company, 32
  consideration for, 71
  decision-making and, 71
  private, 63, 69
oxytocin hormone, 119

P

Parker Clay LLC, 38
patient capital, 140
Peaceful Fruits LLC, 33–34
personal liability, 71
personal story branding, 113
personnel, 94
Pigneur, Y., 55
political system, 30, 32
private ownership, 63, 69
problem identification, 47
problems. *See* social problems
problem-solving, 100
process, of entrepreneurial
 storytelling, 111
profit and loss (P&L) statement, 80
profit distribution, 72
profit margin, 81
profit maximization, 62
program-related investments
 (PRI), 69, 141
public accountability, 67

R

REBOOT, 21–22
RecycleForce, 109
ReFED, 33
religion and worldview, impact of,
 36–37
remote teams, 99
results-based reporting, 85
Retail Food Waste Action Guide, 33
Rethreaded (nonprofit organization), 93
return on assets (ROA), 81
return on equity, 79, 81
return on investment, 96
revenue, 45
revenue generation, 103